365 Day

The Happy Heart Journal

Lindsay Rielly

Post Hill
PRESS

A POST HILL PRESS BOOK
ISBN: 978-1-64293-752-7

The Happy Heart Journal:
365 Days of Happy
© 2021 by Lindsay Rielly
All Rights Reserved

Cover art by Cody Corcoran
Cover Happy Heart inspired by the work of Royce Rielly
Interior design and layout by Sarah Heneghan, sarah-heneghan.com

Although every effort has been made to ensure that the personal and professional advice present within this book is useful and appropriate, the author and publisher do not assume and hereby disclaim any liability to any person, business, or organization choosing to employ the guidance offered in this book.

No part of this book may be reproduced, stored in a retrieval system, or transmitted by any means without the written permission of the author and publisher.

Post Hill Press
New York • Nashville
posthillpress.com

Published in the United States of America
1 2 3 4 5 6 7 8 9 10

To my husband Brennan, whose unfailing love fuels my heart and whose unyielding belief and encouragement allow me to soar. ♥

To my son Royce, who was the inspiration that led me to create this journal and whose wisdom & joy never cease to astound me. ♥

To my stepdaughter Ava, whose openness and conversations have been such a treasured gift in my life. ♥

To my stepdaughter Marlo, whose spunky energy always makes me smile and helped to keep me motivated while writing this in quarantine. ♥

To my Mom & Dad, who have always believed in me, never doubted me, and have loved me without condition. ♥

To some very special kids—Paxx, Ava, Luca, Sky, Helena, Ali, Aleeah, and Addie. Each of you were bright lights in my heart as I wrote this journal. ♥

Finally, thank you, Leah, Tiara, Brian, Leila, Lori, Grampy, Maureen, Matt, and Tom for being pillars of support in my life and throughout this project. ♥

Introduction

Little did I know that when I started to write this journal our world would be hit with the Covid-19 pandemic, a.k.a. coronavirus. I had no idea that I would be writing while in quarantine with four other people in my household. Nor would I have ever thought I would be writing this entire journal on an iPhone from my future husband's house! But part of living a happy life is choosing to be flexible and grateful despite our circumstances. It is understanding that we cannot control what happens outside of us, but we can control how we respond to life. It was challenging at times juggling the responsibilities at home and running my business—all while being fully immersed and emotionally present as I created this journal for all of you.

My mission with this journal was always to provide a roadmap for each of you to connect with your heart, find self-acceptance, recognize your worth, and empower your future, all while being emotionally centered from within. My mission remains the same; however, the purpose of this journal has become even stronger. The world is realizing just how important emotional literacy is. Research has continued to show that emotional well-being is a greater determinant for success than any other form of education.

A Happy Heart is a heart that accepts and embraces all of one's feelings without judgement. A Happy Heart is one that is self-loving and kind. A Happy Heart is compassionate and thoughtful. A Happy Heart is powerful yet peaceful. A Happy Heart understands that there will be good days and not so good days yet is confident that each day offers an opportunity to grow. A Happy Heart is able to ask for help when needed and offer support when another is in need. A Happy Heart is a place of security and optimism. A Happy Heart doesn't just survive, it thrives.

The simple prompts in this journal will inspire personal wellness, purpose, and productivity as you connect with your Happy Heart. You will discover the power of expressing your feelings, preferences, and thoughts. The outside world will no longer have a stronghold on your life and instead you will be able to respond to your environment in beneficial ways. You will activate a sense of self-acceptance and in turn experience greater positivity, joy, and love, which can only be found from within. Happiness is the epicenter of creation and the secret to living an abundant life. By using this journal daily, you will start creating the future you want to live.

I truly believe that each of you has the power to change the world, but it all starts from the changes you make within. My heart is so happy that I get to help each of you become your very best selves. I am so very thankful that I chose to create this for each of you! And it is for YOU!

Day #1

1. What are you hoping to achieve by doing the *Happy Heart Journal*?

_____

_____

2. When do you feel your best?

_____

_____

3. How can you make tomorrow even better than today?

_____

_____

4. Are there any areas of your life that you would like to improve on? Explain what they are and why you want to improve them.

_____

_____

_____

5. What are the 5 things that you are most grateful for today?

_____

_____

♡ Happy Heart Tip: By setting an intention for tomorrow you are essentially creating an emotional goal and putting energy toward it. This will help you to go through each day with more ease and purpose.

Tomorrow I choose (For Example: Tomorrow I choose to be happy): ♡

_____

_____

Day #2

1. What are 3 of your best memories with your loved ones?

_____

_____

_____

2. What makes these memories stand out to you? Explain.

_____

_____

_____

3. Is there anyone in your life who you need to forgive? Who and why?

_____

_____

4. Do you feel that forgiveness is important? Explain.

_____

_____

_____

5. What are the 5 things that you are most grateful for today?

_____

_____

Tomorrow I choose (For Example: Tomorrow I choose to be kind):

_____

Day #3

1. On a scale of 1 to 10 (10 being the best), how would you rate your self-esteem?

_____

_____

2. What habit could you develop that would help improve your self-esteem? Explain.

_____

_____

_____

3. What is a self-defeating thought that you are choosing to let go of today?

_____

_____

_____

4. How does it feel to release thoughts that do not serve your well-being?

_____

_____

_____

5. What are the 5 things that you are most grateful for today?

_____

_____

Tomorrow I choose (For Example: Tomorrow I choose to be generous):

_____

Day #4

1. What did you enjoy most about your day and why?

_____

_____

2. Who is one of your closest friends, and what are 3 of his/her best qualities? ♡

_____

_____

_____

3. What in your life is causing you fear? Explain.

_____

_____

_____

4. How can you reword your fearful thought into a faith-filled statement?

_____

_____

5. What are the 5 things that you are most grateful for today?

_____

_____

Tomorrow I choose (For Example: Tomorrow I choose to be thankful):

_____

_____

♡ Tip: Compliment a friend today. Kindness is a sure way to stay happy heart centered.

Day #5

1. What social media post has inspired you the most and why?

_____

_____

2. List 10 adjectives that best describe you: ♡

1. I am: _____   6. I am: _____

2. I am: _____   7. I am: _____

3. I am: _____   8. I am: _____

4. I am: _____   9. I am: _____

5. I am: _____   10. I am: _____

3. How do you feel when you look at your positive qualities?

_____

4. What is your favorite quality about yourself and why?

_____

_____

5. What are the 5 things that you are most grateful for today?

_____

_____

Tomorrow I choose (For Example: Tomorrow I choose to look at the positives):

♡ Tip: Write your "I am" statements on a piece of paper and post them somewhere you can see them daily. This will keep your happy heart centered.

_____

_____

Day #6

1. What is your heart saying to you today?

_____

_____

2. How do you feel in this moment as you listen to your heart? Explain.

_____

_____

_____

3. What is something that you learned about yourself today?

_____

_____

_____

4. What is one wish that, if granted, would make tomorrow better?

_____

_____

_____

5. What are the 5 things that you are most grateful for today?

_____

_____

Tomorrow I choose:

_____

Day #7

1. What qualities are you most proud of exhibiting today? Explain.

_____

_____

2. What are 5 ways that you demonstrated goodness today?

1. _____

2. _____

3. _____

4. _____

5. _____

3. If you could help one person today or tomorrow who would it be and why?

_____

_____

4. What is a memory that makes you feel good to think about? Explain with detail.

_____

_____

5. What are the 5 things that you are most grateful for today?

_____

_____

Tomorrow I choose:

_____

Day #8

1. When does your heart feel the most full?

_____

_____

2. What does your heart feel like when it is full? Use at least 4 adjectives in your description.

_____

_____

_____

3. What is a positive way that you deal with difficult emotions? Explain. ♡

_____

_____

4. How does it feel when you are able to accept your difficult emotions in a positive way?

_____

_____

5. What are the 5 things that you are most grateful for today?

_____

_____

_____

Tomorrow I choose:

_____

_____

♡ Tip: Close your eyes, name your feeling and where it is located in your body. Put your hand over your heart and say: "I accept that I feel (insert feeling)." Visualize the feeling going into your heart. Repeat this until you can feel that the emotion has been accepted in your heart.

Day #9

1. What makes you a caring friend?

_____

_____

2. What motivates you the most and why?

_____

_____

_____

3. Would you consider yourself more self-focused or other-focused? Explain.

_____

_____

_____

4. When do you feel your happiest? Explain in detail. ♡

_____

_____

5. What are the 5 things that you are most grateful for today?

_____

_____

♡ Tip: Identify when you feel your best. What are you doing? Who are you with? Surround yourself with uplifting, positive people and activities.

Tomorrow I choose:

_____

_____

Day #10

1. What is your greatest vision for your adult life?

_____

_____

2. How do you feel when you envision the life you want to live as an adult?

_____

_____

_____

3. What is one area that you are working on improving in your life?

_____

_____

_____

4. If you could have any superpower, what would it be and how would having it improve your life?

_____

_____

_____

5. What are the 5 things that you are most grateful for today?

_____

_____

Tomorrow I choose:

_____

Day #11

1. What was the best choice you made today? Explain why.

_____

_____

2. What is something that you could have chosen to do differently today?

_____

_____

_____

3. How will you do it differently next time?

_____

_____

_____

4. Would you consider yourself a good decision maker? Explain why or why not.

_____

_____

_____

5. What are the 5 things that you are most grateful for today?

_____

_____

Tomorrow I choose:

_____

Day #12

1. What happened today that was unexpectedly great?

_____

_____

2. What is something that you want to accomplish over the next 7 days?

_____

_____

3. What are 3 things that you can visualize yourself accomplishing over the next 6 months? ♡

1. _____

2. _____

3. _____

4. What are your greatest character strengths? List them out:

1. I am: _____   4. I am: _____

2. I am: _____   5. I am: _____

3. I am: _____

5. What are the 5 things that you are most grateful for today?

_____

_____

Tomorrow I choose:

_____

♡ Tip: Quiet your mind and allow yourself to see these accomplishments as you visualize. Whatever you believe, you can achieve!

Day #13

1. When you close your eyes and picture your heart, what does it look like and how does it feel?

_____

_____

_____

2. Would you like to improve how your heart feels today? Explain with detail.

_____

_____

3. Where are you struggling in your heart today?

_____

_____

4. What are 5 positive qualities about your heart? ♡

1. _____   4. _____

2. _____   5. _____

3. _____

5. What are the 5 things that you are most grateful for today?

_____

_____

♡ Tip: Focus on what feels good and the good feeling will get better. Acknowledge what does not feel good with acceptance, but do not spend your time focused there. Whatever you spend your energy on increases.

Tomorrow I choose:

_____

_____

Day #14

1. My 5 goals for tomorrow are:

1. _____   4. _____

2. _____   5. _____

3. _____

2. What is the last goal you can remember achieving and how did it feel to accomplish it? Give details.

_____

_____

_____

3. Are you hard on yourself when you feel like you have underachieved? Explain why or why not.

_____

_____

4. How could you be more accepting of yourself? Explain.

_____

_____

5. What are the 5 things that you are most grateful for today?

_____

_____

Tomorrow I choose:

_____

Day #15

1. If you could make one positive thing happen tomorrow what would it be and why?

_____

_____

_____

2. What would it feel like to have this happen?

_____

_____

_____

3. What has been your most valuable lesson that you learned over the past year, and what did you learn from it?

_____

_____

_____

4. What was something that recently seemed "bad" but turned out good? Explain.

_____

_____

5. What are the 5 things that you are most grateful for today?

_____

_____

Tomorrow I choose:

_____

Day #16

1. What does it mean to be a good friend? Explain.

_____

_____

_____

2. How did you exhibit friendship today?

_____

_____

3. If you could help one person, who would it be and why?

_____

_____

_____

4. How would you like to feel better supported in your life?

_____

_____

_____

5. What are the 5 things that you are most grateful for today?

_____

_____

Tomorrow I choose:

_____

Day #17

1. When do you believe that you at your very best? Explain.

_____

_____

2. What qualities are you most proud of exhibiting today?

1. I am: _____   6. I am: _____

2. I am: _____   7. I am: _____

3. I am: _____   8. I am: _____

4. I am: _____   9. I am: _____

5. I am: _____   10. I am: _____

3. What does being in alignment mean to you?

_____

_____

4. What is your vision for your life for the rest of the year? Explain in detail.

_____

_____

5. What are the 5 things that you are most grateful for today?

_____

_____

Tomorrow I choose:

_____

Day #18

1. What qualities do people most often tell you that they see in you?

_____

_____

2. How do you feel when you receive positive affirmations?

_____

_____

_____

3. What prayer or positive thought can you express today that will influence your future in a powerful way? Give detail.

_____

_____

_____

4. What activities do you enjoy the most?

_____

_____

_____

5. What are the 5 things that you are most grateful for today?

_____

_____

Tomorrow I choose:

_____

Day #19

1. What are you most proud to have accomplished today?

_____

_____

_____

2. On a scale of 1 to 10 (10 being the best), how would you rate your attitude today and why?

_____

_____

3. What are you committed to doing tomorrow to make it an even better day? Explain.

_____

_____

_____

4. How would you describe your life in 5 words?

1. _____   4. _____

2. _____   5. _____

3. _____

5. What are the 5 things that you are most grateful for today?

_____

_____

Tomorrow I choose:

_____

Day #20

1. What 3 positive qualities do you see growing in you?

1. _____

2. _____

3. _____

2. If you could grant one wish for someone, what would it be and why?

_____

_____

_____

3. What are your 5 strongest character traits?

1. _____

2. _____

3. _____

4. _____

5. _____

4. What is something you would like to improve in your life today?

Physically: _____

_____

Spiritually: _____

_____

(continued on the next page...)

Day #20, continued

Mentally:

_____

_____

5. What are the 5 things that you are most grateful for today?

_____

_____

Tomorrow I choose:

_____

_____

Day #21

1. What did you love most about today and why?

_____

_____

_____

2. How did you improve your life today?

_____

_____

_____

3. When you are happy, how does your heart feel?

_____

_____

4. What have you learned about yourself while doing this journal so far? Explain.

_____

_____

_____

5. What are the 5 things that you are most grateful for today?

_____

_____

Tomorrow I choose:

_____

Day #22

1. What behavior would make you know without a doubt that you are loved?

_____

_____

2. What is one area of your thinking that you would like to improve?

_____

_____

3. What is a way that you have observed your thinking improve since starting this journal?

_____

_____

_____

4. What are you most excited for and why?

_____

_____

_____

5. What are the 5 things that you are most grateful for today?

_____

_____

Tomorrow I choose:

_____

Day #23

1. When do you feel most comforted and encouraged?

_____

_____

2. How does it feel to be comforted and encouraged?

_____

_____

_____

3. Who do you feel most comforted and encouraged by and why?

_____

_____

_____

4. What person has made the biggest impact on your life and how?

_____

_____

_____

5. What are the 5 things that you are most grateful for today?

_____

_____

Tomorrow I choose:

_____

Day #24

1. How do you support yourself when you are feeling down?

_____

_____

2. Do you feel lonely when you are down? Explain why or why not.

_____

_____

3. What do you like most about your life? Explain. ♡

_____

_____

_____

4. What small change are you willing to make today that will improve your life? Explain.

_____

_____

_____

5. What are the 5 things that you are most grateful for today?

_____

_____

♡ Tip: At times life feels tough and it can be challenging to find the positive. In these moments find something that you are thankful for regardless of how big or small it is. This will instantly help you appreciate your life outside of your circumstances.

Tomorrow I choose:

_____

_____

Day #25

1. How did you stay connected to your happy heart today?

_____

_____

2. How do you feel when you are in your happy heart compared to when you are not? Explain.

_____

_____

_____

3. What is a positive way that you chose to handle a challenge today?

_____

_____

4. What physical activity did you engage in today? Did you enjoy it? Why or why not.

_____

_____

_____

_____

5. What are the 5 things that you are most grateful for today?

_____

_____

Tomorrow I choose:

_____

Day #26

1. How did you spread kindness today?

_____

_____

_____

2. How does being kind feel to you? Explain.

_____

_____

_____

3. If you could take one person and one item with you while stranded on an island, who would you take and what item would you bring?

_____

_____

4. What was the best thing that happened today, and what was the most difficult?

_____

_____

_____

5. What are the 5 things that you are most grateful for today?

_____

_____

Tomorrow I choose:

_____

Day #27

1. What does happiness feel like to you?

1. Happiness feels: _____

2. Happiness feels: _____

3. Happiness feels: _____

4. Happiness feels: _____

5. Happiness feels: _____

2. What made you smile the biggest today? Give details.

_____

_____

3. Fill in the blank. I am exceptional because:

_____

_____

4. How does it feel to recognize your super strengths?

_____

_____

5. What are the 5 things that you are most grateful for today?

_____

_____

Tomorrow I choose:

_____

Day #28

1. What was the best part of your day today? Explain.

_____

_____

_____

2. How are you learning to stay connected to your happy heart? Give an example.

_____

_____

_____

3. When faced with a challenge, what is a new and positive way that you have chosen to deal with it?

_____

_____

_____

4. When do you feel your best?

_____

_____

5. What are the 5 things that you are most grateful for today?

_____

_____

Tomorrow I choose:

_____

Day #29

1. What do you respect about yourself?

_____

_____

2. What does respecting yourself look like in action?

_____

_____

_____

3. How do you feel when you respect yourself? Explain.

_____

_____

_____

4. Did you show respect to others today? Explain why or why not.

_____

_____

_____

5. What are the 5 things that you are most grateful for today?

_____

_____

Tomorrow I choose:

_____

Day #30

1. How did you exercise kindness today?

_____

_____

2. What are some ways that you deal with challenges that do not serve your best interest? Explain.

_____

_____

_____

3. What are a couple more positive coping mechanisms that you could use when dealing with challenges? ♡

_____

_____

4. What 3 things are you looking most forward to over the next few days?

1._____ 3._____

2._____

5. What are the 5 things that you are most grateful for today?

_____

♡ Tip: Anytime you're dealing with a challenge and overthinking it; take a deep breath, inhaling for 4 seconds, holding the breath for 6 seconds, and exhaling for 8 seconds. Repeat until you feel calm. Thoughts do not exist when you are in the act of a breath.

Tomorrow I choose:

_____

_____

Day #31

1. What are 3 ways that you felt blessed today?

1. _____

2. _____

3. _____

2. What is your greatest blessing in life and why?

_____

_____

_____

3. What is a quality that you have that you are most proud of and why?

_____

_____

_____

4. How does it feel to bestow this quality?

_____

_____

5. What are the 5 things that you are most grateful for today?

_____

_____

Tomorrow I choose:

_____

Day #32

1. How did you overcome a struggle or fear today?

_____

_____

2. How did it feel to overcome this challenge?

_____

_____

_____

3. From a 1 to 10 (10 being the ultimate) how would you rate your self-esteem? Explain your answer.

_____

_____

_____

4. What are 3 ways that you are committed to improving your self-confidence?

_____

_____

_____

5. What are the 5 things that you are most grateful for today?

_____

_____

Tomorrow I choose:

_____

Day #33

1. Who inspired you today and how were you inspired?

_____

_____

_____

2. How were you an inspiration today and how did it impact others?

_____

_____

_____

3. When you feel inspired, how does your energy shift?

_____

_____

_____

4. What are you most looking forward to tomorrow?

_____

_____

5. What are the 5 things that you are most grateful for today?

_____

_____

Tomorrow I choose:

_____

Day #34

1. Would you consider yourself optimistic? Explain why or why not?

_____

_____

_____

2. What is something that you are struggling to look at with optimism?

_____

_____

3. How can you choose to shift that thought pattern to your benefit?

_____

_____

_____

4. What is one way that you thought optimistically today? Explain how it impacted your day.

_____

_____

_____

5. What are the 5 things that you are most grateful for today?

_____

_____

Tomorrow I choose:

_____

Day #35

1. Do you find it difficult to admit when you are wrong? Explain why or why not?

_____

_____

_____

2. What feelings come up for you when you realize that you are wrong?

_____

_____

3. Do you believe that being wrong is a bad thing? ♡

_____

_____

4. Do you have someone in your life who is regularly able to admit when they are wrong? How have they influenced you?

_____

_____

_____

5. What are the 5 things that you are most grateful for today?

_____

_____

Tomorrow I choose:

_____

_____

♡ Tip: Everyone is imperfect and bound to be wrong at times. It is in your ability to admit when you are mistaken; that shows a strength in your character. Pride and ego can destroy relationships and opportunities. In learning to say "my bad," "I was wrong," or even "I'm sorry," you find great power and confidence.

Day #36

1. When was the last time you got mad at someone and what happened?

_____

_____

_____

2. How did you deal with this feeling?

_____

_____

3. Do you feel that you handle anger in a healthy way? Why or why not?

_____

_____

_____

4. What are a few ways that you could handle your anger in a healthier way? Explain.

_____

_____

_____

5. What are the 5 things that you are most grateful for today?

_____

_____

Tomorrow I choose:

_____

Day #37

1. What do you worry about the most?

_____

_____

2. What are 3 ways you combat worried thoughts?

1. _____

2. _____

3. _____

3. What optimistic thoughts could you use to replace the worried ones?

_____

_____

_____

4. What is something that you did today that felt really good? Explain.

_____

_____

_____

5. What are the 5 things that you are most grateful for today?

_____

_____

Tomorrow I choose:

_____

Day #38

1. Are you able to express and share your feelings with others? Explain why or why not. ♡

_____

_____

2. How would you like to improve on how you express yourself to others? Explain.

_____

_____

3. Do you feel uncomfortable expressing yourself to your friends and loved ones? Explain why or why not.

_____

_____

♡ Tip: It is important to be able to express what you are feeling even if the feeling feels yucky. Remember feelings are not right or wrong, they are your experience and your truth. When expressing your feelings to others, start by addressing what it was that happened that caused you to feel a certain way, and follow it with your identified feeling(s)—for example: Mom, when you said you didn't believe me, I felt hurt and not trusted. Or another example could be: Dad, when you told me you were proud of me, it made me feel happy; thank you. Both expressions are extremely positive because you are choosing to honor yourself without judgement of another.

4. How do you respond when someone expresses displeasure with you?

_____

_____

_____

5. What are the 5 things that you are most grateful for today?

_____

_____

Tomorrow I choose:

_____

Day #39

1. How did you listen well today? Give an example. ♡

_____

_____

_____

2. What did you learn while listening today?

_____

_____

3. How did you adapt to something unexpected today?

_____

_____

4. How do you feel dealing with unexpected events? Explain.

_____

_____

_____

5. What are the 5 things that you are most grateful for today?

_____

_____

Tomorrow I choose:

_____

_____

♡ Tip: Listening to learn is an essential quality for success in all aspects of life. When you listen to respond, you're not actually listening; you are thinking about the future instead of hearing what is being said in the present. Practice listening to learn and watch how connected you feel.

Day #40

1. What is one way that you improved yourself today?

_____

_____

2. How do you feel when you observe yourself improving? Explain.

_____

_____

_____

3. What do you like best about your life and why?

_____

_____

_____

4. What is a recent improvement that you have made in your thinking and how has it impacted your daily life?

_____

_____

_____

5. What are the 5 things that you are most grateful for today?

_____

_____

Tomorrow I choose:

_____

Day #41

1. When did you feel most loved today?

_____

_____

2. How does it feel when you are feeling loved by others?

_____

_____

_____

3. When you tap into your happy heart right now, what adjectives would you use to describe yourself?

1. I am: _____   4. I am: _____

2. I am: _____   5. I am: _____

3. I am: _____

4. What do find to be the biggest challenge of being a kid, tween, or teen?

_____

_____

_____

5. What are the 5 things that you are most grateful for today?

_____

_____

Tomorrow I choose:

_____

Day #42

1. What fear would you like to conquer and why?

_____

_____

2. Do you feel motivated by your fears or paralyzed by them? Explain.

_____

_____

_____

3. What is one small thing that you can do tomorrow to face your fear with confidence? Explain.

_____

_____

_____

4. What is one fear that you have overcome in your life? How did it feel to overcome it?

_____

_____

_____

5. What are the 5 things that you are most grateful for today?

_____

_____

Tomorrow I choose:

_____

Day #43

1. What kind of life are you committed to creating?

_____

_____

2. How does it feel to know that you get to design your life? Explain.

_____

_____

_____

3. When do you feel most confident?

_____

_____

_____

4. Did you feel confident today? Explain why or why not.

_____

_____

_____

5. What are the 5 things that you are most grateful for today?

_____

_____

Tomorrow I choose:

_____

Day #44

1. What do you do consistently that has helped you become successful in an area of your life?

_____

_____

2. What could you do more consistently that would benefit your goals?

_____

_____

3. Do you believe it is important to have goals at your age? Explain why or why not.

_____

_____

_____

4. If you could achieve one thing that seems impossible, what would it be and how would achieving it feel?

_____

_____

_____

5. What are the 5 things that you are most grateful for today?

_____

_____

Tomorrow I choose:

_____

Day #45

1. What is your favorite way to spend quality time with loved ones?

_____

_____

_____

2. How do you feel when you are spending quality time with loved ones?

_____

_____

3. What is one way that you contributed to making the world a better place this week?

_____

_____

_____

4. If you could go anywhere in the world with one person, where would you go and who would you take with you?

_____

_____

_____

5. What are the 5 things that you are most grateful for today?

_____

_____

Tomorrow I choose:

_____

Day #46

1. Who are your biggest cheerleaders in life and why?

_____

_____

2. How does it feel to have supportive people in your life? Explain.

_____

_____

_____

3. When you are sad, are you able to share your feelings with a trusted family member or friend?

_____

_____

_____

4. What could help you to be even more open with your feelings? Explain.

_____

_____

_____

5. What are the 5 things that you are most grateful for today?

_____

_____

Tomorrow I choose:

_____

Day #47

1. What are your 5 favorite personality traits?

1. _____   4. _____

2. _____   5. _____

3. _____

2. How do you feel when you feel understood by others? Use at least one sentence to describe.

_____

_____

3. How do you feel when you don't feel understood by others? Use at least one sentence to describe.

_____

_____

4. What are 3 ways that you could communicate your needs better?

1. _____

2. _____

3. _____

5. What are the 5 things that you are most grateful for today?

_____

_____

Tomorrow I choose:

_____

Day #48

1. What are 10 positive qualities about yourself that feel great to you?

1. I am: _____

2. I am: _____

3. I am: _____

4. I am: _____

5. I am: _____

6. I am: _____

7. I am: _____

8. I am: _____

9. I am: _____

10. I am: _____

2. How do you feel when you acknowledge your positive qualities? Explain.

_____

_____

3. What are you most excited for tomorrow?

_____

_____

4. What person inspires you to be a better person and why?

_____

_____

5. What are the 5 things that you are most grateful for today?

_____

_____

Tomorrow I choose:

_____

Day #49

1. How did you take responsibility today? Explain.

_____

_____

2. How does it feel when you are being responsible? Describe with at least 2 adjectives.

_____

_____

3. Do you find it difficult to apologize?

_____

4. Is there anyone who you need to apologize to? If so what would you like to say to that person? ♡

_____

_____

5. Recall a time that you received an apology. Who was it from? What did they say and how did it feel to hear their remorse?

_____

_____

6. What are the 5 things that you are most grateful for today?

_____

_____

Tomorrow I choose:

_____

_____

> ♡ Tip: Apologizing when you are wrong or when you have hurt someone is a way to build back trust and understanding with the other person. Don't be afraid to let someone know that you are sorry.

Day #50

1. What is one way that you acted lovingly today?

_____

_____

2. How do you feel when you act lovingly to others? Explain.

_____

_____

_____

3. When is a time that you chose to be honest even though it was hard? What happened?

_____

_____

_____

4. Is being honest challenging for you? Why or why not.

_____

_____

_____

5. What are the 5 things that you are most grateful for today?

_____

_____

Tomorrow I choose:

_____

Day #51

1. What rule could you create that would have a positive impact at your school or in your home?

_____

_____

2. What is the best way for your loved ones to express their love for you?

_____

_____

3. When your loved ones express their love for you, how does it make you feel?

_____

_____

4. How do you feel when you express love to your loved ones? Explain. ♡

_____

_____

_____

5. What are the 5 things that you are most grateful for today?

_____

_____

Tomorrow I choose:

_____

_____

♡ Tip: Expressing love can bring up a lot of feelings. Don't be hard on yourself if, when expressing love, you feel awkward. It is perfectly normal to feel uncomfortable when being vulnerable with others. The key is to be brave. Sharing your feelings of love and appreciation will get easier as you grow.

Day #52

1. Did you have a good day or not so good day today? Explain.

_____

_____

2. How did you honor your feelings today?

_____

_____

3. How do you feel when you honor your feelings? Use at least one sentence to explain.

_____

_____

_____

4. When did you feel at your best today?

_____

_____

_____

5. What are the 5 things that you are most grateful for today?

_____

_____

_____

Tomorrow I choose:

_____

Day #53

1. How were you a good friend today?

_____

_____

_____

2. What is a behavior that annoys you?

_____

_____

3. How do you respond when you feel annoyed?

_____

_____

_____

4. Do you believe that your response is effective? Explain why or why not.

_____

_____

_____

5. What are the 5 things that you are most grateful for today?

_____

_____

Tomorrow I choose:

_____

Day #54

1. How have you bounced back from a setback? Explain.

_____

_____

_____

2. What do you consider your 10 most significant strengths?

1. _____

2. _____

3. _____

4. _____

5. _____

6. _____

7. _____

8. _____

9. _____

10. _____

3. How do your greatest strengths benefit you in your life?

_____

_____

_____

(continued on the next page...)

Day #54, continued

4. How does it feel to look at your strengths? Use at least 3 adjectives to explain.

_____

_____

_____

_____

5. What are the 5 things that you are most grateful for today?

_____

_____

_____

Tomorrow I choose:

_____

_____

Day #55

1. What was awesome about today?

_____

_____

2. What do you like about focusing on the good of the day as opposed to the not so good?

_____

_____

_____

3. Is there anything that you did today that you feel badly about?

_____

_____

_____

4. When is the last time that you cried and why? ♡

_____

_____

5. What are the 5 things that you are most grateful for today?

♡ Tip: Be proud of yourself for being able to express sadness. Remember to also work on accepting it. Crying is known to be self-soothing and a way to reduce emotional pain and promote well-being. If you feel like crying, accept your sadness and do not be ashamed for expressing it.

_____

_____

Tomorrow I choose:

_____

_____

Day #56

1. What is something that you know how to do that you could teach to others?

_____

_____

_____

2. What is something that you would like to learn to do from someone you know?

_____

_____

_____

3. What are the best and worst things that have happened to you?

_____

_____

_____

4. What did you learn from these best and worst experiences that you have lived?

_____

_____

5. What are the 5 things that you are most grateful for today?

_____

_____

Tomorrow I choose:

_____

Day #57

1. Of all the things that you are learning about yourself while doing this journal, what are the 3 that you feel will be the most useful in your adult life?

_____

_____

2. How did you exhibit compassion today? Use at least one sentence to explain.

_____

_____

_____

3. How does it feel to show compassion to others? Use at least 3 adjectives to describe.

_____

_____

_____

4. How could you make improvements in your attitude that would positively impact tomorrow?

_____

_____

5. What are the 5 things that you are most grateful for today?

_____

_____

Tomorrow I choose:

_____

Day #58

1. How did you incorporate generosity into your day?

_____

_____

2. How does it feel to be generous?

_____

_____

_____

3. What was the best moment of today?

_____

_____

4. What are you willing to commit to for tomorrow?

_____

_____

5. What made you feel happy today?

_____

_____

6. What are the 5 things that you are most grateful for today?

_____

_____

Tomorrow I choose:

_____

Day #59

1. What color do you believe is the happiest color? What makes it happy? Describe.

_____

_____

_____

2. What color is the saddest color? What makes it sad? Explain.

_____

_____

3. What color do you relate to most and why?

_____

_____

_____

4. What color is your heart today? Use 3 adjectives to describe how that color feels.

_____

_____

_____

5. What are the 5 things that you are most grateful for today?

_____

_____

Tomorrow I choose:

_____

Day #60

1. When was the last time you stuck up for someone? What happened?

_____

_____

_____

2. How does it feel to step up and stick up for someone?

_____

_____

3. Have you ever been teased? What happened and how did it feel?

_____

_____

_____

4. How did you express confidence today?

_____

_____

_____

5. What are the 5 things that you are most grateful for today?

_____

_____

Tomorrow I choose:

_____

Day #61

1. What are 3 things that gave you the most energy today?

1. _____

2. _____

3. _____

2. How does it feel when you have energy throughout the day? Explain.

_____

_____

_____

3. What has surprised you the most about writing in this journal?

_____

_____

4. If you could relive one day all over again, what day would it be and why?

_____

_____

_____

5. What are the 5 things that you are most grateful for today?

_____

_____

Tomorrow I choose:

_____

Day #62

1. How did you manage your time today? Give details of how you managed it well or not so well?

_____

_____

_____

2. How were you a good friend today?

_____

_____

3. What are you looking most forward to in the next couple of weeks and why?

_____

_____

_____

4. What does happiness feel like? Give 5 adjectives to describe it.

1. _____   4. _____

2. _____   5. _____

3. _____

5. What are the 5 things that you are most grateful for today?

_____

_____

Tomorrow I choose:

_____

Day #63

1. What are your 5 best leadership qualities?

1. _____

2. _____

3. _____

4. _____

5. _____

2. Do you enjoy leading others? Explain why or why not.

_____

_____

3. When did you feel most self-confident today?

_____

_____

4. How did feeling confident impact your day?

_____

_____

5. What are the 5 things that you are most grateful for today?

_____

_____

Tomorrow I choose:

_____

Day #64

1. Picture your life a year from now, what do you believe you will congratulate yourself for accomplishing?

_____

_____

_____

2. Who are 2 influential people in your life that you would like to thank and what would you like to say to them?

_____

_____

_____

3. What was the most rewarding part of your day and why?

_____

_____

4. What have you been doing to stay centered in your happy heart? Give at least 2 examples.

_____

_____

5. What are the 5 things that you are most grateful for today?

_____

_____

Tomorrow I choose:

_____

Day #65

1. When did you feel happiest today?

_____

_____

2. Using your 5 senses, what does happiness:

1. Feel like: _____

2. Look like: _____

3. Sound like: _____

4. Taste like: _____

5. Smell like: _____

3. What teacher do you respect the most and why?

_____

_____

4. What is your biggest goal for the next month?

_____

_____

5. What are the 5 things that you are most grateful for today?

_____

_____

Tomorrow I choose:

_____

Day #66

1. How would you describe your personality?

_____

_____

2. What do you appreciate most about your personality and what would you like to improve upon?

_____

_____

_____

3. How would you describe the personality of your best friend? In your opinion, what is their very best quality?

_____

_____

_____

4. When did you feel the most loved today?

_____

_____

5. What are the 5 things that you are most grateful for today?

_____

_____

Tomorrow I choose:

_____

Day #67

1. What do you wish that you had been motivated to do today?

_____

_____

2. How can you increase your motivation to be more effective in reaching your goals?

_____

_____

3. Did you stay in your happy heart today? Explain.

_____

_____

4. What are 3 small yet impactful victories that you have had the past few days that you are proud of?

1. _____

2. _____

3. _____

5. How did you follow through today? Give at least one example.

_____

_____

6. What are the 5 things that you are most grateful for today?

_____

Tomorrow I choose:

_____

Day #68

1.What do you believe are the 5 most important components to living a great life?

1. _____

2. _____

3. _____

4. _____

5. _____

2. Why are these components important to living a great life?

_____

_____

3. How would you explain the word "happiness" to someone, without using the word "happy"?

_____

_____

4. What is one thing that you learned about yourself today?

_____

_____

5. What are the 5 things that you are most grateful for today?

_____

_____

Tomorrow I choose:

_____

Day #69

1. What were the 3 best moments of your day and why?

_____

_____

_____

2. When did you feel the most calm today? What were you doing?

_____

_____

3. Over the past few days, when did you feel down and were you able to accept your feelings or not? Explain.

_____

_____

_____

4. What was the result of either accepting your feelings or not being able to do so?

_____

_____

_____

5. What are the 5 things that you are most grateful for today?

_____

_____

Tomorrow I choose:

_____

Day #70

1. Over the past month, can you recall a time when you said no to doing something that didn't feel right to you? How did you feel standing up for your beliefs?

_____

_____

2. What makes you feel confident in your judgement?

_____

_____

3. What are 5 ways in which you have improved yourself over the past couple of months?

1. _____

2. _____

3. _____

4. _____

5. _____

4. How does it feel to have improved in these areas? Use at least 3 adjectives.

_____

_____

5. What are the 5 things that you are most grateful for today?

_____

_____

Tomorrow I choose:

_____

Day #71

1. Have you felt angry over the past few days? If so, what happened? If not, describe the last time you felt angry and what the situation was.

_____

_____

2. How did you manage your angry feelings?

_____

_____

3. What can you do to improve the way you cope with anger?

_____

_____

4. What are you most proud of yourself for today? Explain.

_____

_____

_____

5. What are the 5 things that you are most grateful for today? ♡

♡ Tip: An attitude of gratitude is one of the surest ways to get back into your happy heart when you're feeling mad, sad, frustrated, annoyed, or any kind of yucky feeling. Shifting your mindset to the positive is a life skill that will never harm you. If possible, focus on what you are thankful for. If that is too hard, look at something that feels good to you.

_____

_____

Tomorrow I choose:

_____

_____

Day #72

1. What does it mean to have a support system?

_____

_____

2. What 3 people do you feel most supported by, and how have they recently shown up for you?

_____

_____

_____

3. How have you been a supportive family member, friend, or student over the past few days? Give 3 examples:

_____

_____

_____

4. Give an example of how you trusted yourself today?

_____

_____

5. What are the 5 things that you are most grateful for today?

_____

_____

Tomorrow I choose:

_____

Day #73

1. What goals have you set and accomplished over the past couple of weeks? Give details.

_____

_____

_____

2. How does accomplishing goals make you feel? Use at least 3 adjectives.

_____

_____

_____

3. What is something that happened today that made you appreciate your life?

_____

_____

_____

4. What are you looking most forward to over the next few days?

_____

_____

5. What are the 5 things that you are most grateful for today?

_____

_____

Tomorrow I choose:

_____

Day #74

1. When you are feeling down, what generally cheers you up?

_____

_____

2. If you visualize your life in 20 years, what does it look like? Write a short paragraph explaining your vision in detail.

_____

_____

_____

3. How did you choose to remain positive today? ♡

_____

_____

4. How can you choose to think differently in a way that will benefit your life?

_____

_____

_____

5. What are the 5 things that you are most grateful for today?

_____

_____

Tomorrow I choose:

_____

_____

♡ Tip: The happiness that you experience depends upon the quality of your thoughts. The more positive your thoughts, the better your day will be.

Day #75

1. How do you see clearly when your life is cloudy? ♡

_____

_____

2. How did you display accountability today?

_____

_____

3. How does it feel when you take responsibility?

_____

_____

_____

4. If you could develop one skill overnight, what would it be and how would it benefit your life?

_____

_____

_____

5. What are the 5 things that you are most grateful for today?

_____

_____

♡ Tip: Remember that the storms of life are an opportunity to grow. Many storms come to clear a path for you to progress, evolve, and find greater clarity.

Tomorrow I choose:

_____

_____

Day #76

1. Do you find yourself comparing your life to others? Explain. ♡

_____

_____

2. How do you feel when you compare yourself to someone else?

_____

_____

_____

3. Are you able to accept the ways in which you are different from others? Explain why or why not.

_____

_____

_____

4. On a scale of 1 to 10 (10 being the highest) how well did you stay connected to your happy heart today?

_____

5. What are the 5 things that you are most grateful for today?

_____

_____

Tomorrow I choose:

_____

_____

♡ Tip: Comparison is the thief of joy. You are a beautiful, unique, and amazing person. Being YOU is your superpower. There's nothing to gain from comparing your life to someone else's.

Day #77

1. When did you feel your best today? Share your experience.

_____

_____

_____

2. When didn't you feel your best today? Share your experience.

_____

_____

_____

3. What tools did you use today to reconnect with your happy heart?

_____

_____

4. What is something that you dream of that encourages you?

_____

_____

_____

5. What are the 5 things that you are most grateful for today?

_____

_____

Tomorrow I choose:

_____

Day #78

1. How do you calm yourself when you get upset? ♡

_____

_____

2. When do you feel most passionate? Give an example.

_____

_____

3. When did you smile today? What were you doing?

_____

_____

4. Give yourself 5 compliments:

1. _____

2. _____

3. _____

4 _____

5. _____

5. What are the 5 things that you are most grateful for today?

_____

_____

Tomorrow I choose:

_____

> ♡ Tip: Take a pause. Stop what you're doing and inhale. When you inhale, imagine smelling something that you love. This could be chocolate chip cookies, pizza, or anything that smells delicious. Exhale whatever tension you're holding in. Do this as many times as you need to get back into your happy heart center.

Day #79

1. If tomorrow you could do anything that you wanted, what would you do? Give details of what you would do from morning to night.

_____

_____

2. What is one thing that you are looking forward to?

_____

_____

3. What 5 things do you appreciate the most about yourself today?

1. _____

2. _____

3. _____

4. _____

5. _____

4. What is one way that you contributed positivity to the world today?

_____

_____

5. What are the 5 things that you are most grateful for today?

_____

_____

Tomorrow I choose:

_____

Day #80

1. Have you felt lonely over the past few days? Explain. ♡

_____

_____

2. How do you feel when you are in connection with others? Use at least 3 adjectives to describe.

_____

_____

3. What surprised you about yourself today?

_____

_____

_____

4. How has your vision for your life changed since starting this journal?

_____

_____

_____

5. What are the 5 things that you are most grateful for today?

_____

_____

Tomorrow I choose:

_____

♡ Tip: Remember, feeling lonely can happen while you are alone or in a room full of people. We are wired for connection, so sometimes when we feel emotionally disconnected, we feel lonely. It is normal and common to feel lonely and it usually passes, however, often asking for support is necessary. If you're feeling lonely, reach out to someone who you can trust for support. This could be a parent, caretaker, counselor, friend, teacher, etc. Connecting with animals can also ease the feeling of loneliness, as can joining an appropriate online support group. Keep journaling and expressing your feelings. Focus on the present moment and try not to jump to the past or future. Accept the feeling. It is normal and natural. Keep participating in activities you enjoy.

Day #81

1. What animal do you feel represents your personality and why?

_____

_____

_____

2. How did you express appreciation today?

_____

_____

_____

3. How did you cope with a challenge today?

_____

_____

_____

4. What are you looking most forward to tomorrow?

_____

_____

5. What are the 5 things that you are most grateful for today?

_____

_____

Tomorrow I choose:

_____

Day #82

1. If you had a canvas in front of you to paint your feelings, what would your painting look like?

_____

_____

2. Using your 5 senses, how would you describe generosity?

1. Generosity smells like: _____

2. Generosity tastes like: _____

3. Generosity looks like: _____

4. Generosity feels like: _____

5. Generosity sounds like: _____

3. What color represents how you feel today and why?

_____

_____

4. What caring behaviors did you exhibit today and how does being caring feel?

_____

_____

5. What are the 5 things that you are most grateful for today?

_____

_____

Tomorrow I choose:

_____

Day #83

1. If you could go anywhere in the world to experience something new, where would you go and what would you do?

_____

_____

_____

2. Who is your role model and why?

_____

_____

_____

3. What has been your proudest moment over the past few days?

_____

_____

_____

4. When did you feel at your best today? Explain. ♡

_____

_____

5. What are the 5 things that you are most grateful for today?

_____

_____

♡ Tip: When you know what feels good to you, you're able to recreate it again and again.

Tomorrow I choose:

_____

Day #84

1. What has been your favorite age. Explain why you loved this time in your life.

_____

_____

_____

2. Did you struggle with anything today? If so, how did you cope with it? If not, how do you generally deal with adversity?

_____

_____

_____

3. What do you feel you did well today?

_____

_____

_____

4. What do you feel you want to work on improving tomorrow?

_____

_____

5. What are the 5 things that you are most grateful for today?

_____

_____

Tomorrow I choose:

_____

Day #85

1. What is on your mind right now? Get it all out!

_____

_____

_____

_____

2. How could you improve your mindset in this moment? Share some ideas.

_____

_____

_____

3. When did you feel the most peaceful today? Explain.

_____

_____

4. What are you most proud of yourself for today?

_____

_____

5. What are the 5 things that you are most grateful for today?

_____

_____

Tomorrow I choose:

_____

Day #86

1. How were you courageous today?

_____

_____

2. How does it feel to be courageous? Scary? Liberating? A combination of both? Explain.

_____

_____

_____

3. What does it mean to honor yourself?

_____

_____

_____

4. Give an example of a time that you honored yourself and share how you felt.

_____

_____

_____

5. What are the 5 things that you are most grateful for today?

_____

_____

Tomorrow I choose:

_____

Day #87

1. If you could choose to be loved or respected, which one would you choose and why?

_____

_____

_____

2. What does being loved feel like to you?

_____

_____

3. What does being respected feel like to you?

_____

_____

_____

4. If you could change one thing about today, what would you change and why?

_____

_____

_____

5. What are the 5 things that you are most grateful for today?

_____

_____

Tomorrow I choose:

_____

Day #88

1. When life gets tough, what generally lifts your mood?

_____

_____

_____

2. How did you make healthy choices today? What happened?

_____

_____

_____

3. In what moments could you have made better or healthier choices?

_____

_____

4. If you could spend one day as anyone you know, who would it be and why would you want to be this person for the day?

_____

_____

_____

5. What are the 5 things that you are most grateful for today?

_____

_____

Tomorrow I choose:

_____

Day #89

1. What is the biggest obstacle that you have overcome over the last year? Explain in detail.

_____

_____

_____

_____

2. How did it feel to overcome such a challenge?

_____

_____

_____

3. How did you spread kindness today?

_____

_____

4. What does it feel like when you are kind to others?

_____

_____

5. What are the 5 things that you are most grateful for today?

_____

_____

Tomorrow I choose:

_____

Day #90

1. What was your proudest moment today? Explain what happened.

_____

_____

_____

2. Who do you rely on most when you are feeling down?

_____

_____

_____

3. What makes this person dependable?

_____

_____

4. When is the last time that you reached out for help and what happened?

_____

_____

_____

5. What are the 5 things that you are most grateful for today?

_____

_____

Tomorrow I choose:

_____

Day #91

1. What does positivity feel like?

_____

_____

2. What did you do today to increase your overall sense of well-being?

_____

_____

_____

3. What does it mean to have a purpose in life? Explain.

_____

_____

_____

4. In thinking about your own life, what is a purpose that you feel you have? If you don't know, what is something that you are passionate about that could inspire a purpose?

_____

_____

_____

5. What are the 5 things that you are most grateful for today?

_____

_____

Tomorrow I choose:

_____

Day #92

1. Did anything upset you today? If so, what happened? If not, share something that has upset you over the past few days.

_____

_____

2. How did you find resolution to whatever it was that upset you? If you are still upset, what is something that you can do within the next 24 hours to help resolve the situation?

_____

_____

_____

3. If you could buy one person a special present, who would it be and what would you give them?

_____

_____

4. What did you improve about yourself today?

_____

_____

5. What are the 5 things that you are most grateful for today?

_____

_____

Tomorrow I choose:

_____

Day #93

1. What are your 10 best character traits?

1. I am: _____   6. I am: _____

2. I am: _____   7. I am: _____

3. I am: _____   8. I am: _____

4. I am: _____   9. I am: _____

5. I am: _____   10. I am: _____

2. What do you feel like when you focus on your positive qualities? Explain.

_____

_____

3. How did you express yourself in a healthy way today? What happened?

_____

_____

4. Who would you like to thank and why do they deserve appreciation?

_____

_____

5. What are the 5 things that you are most grateful for today?

_____

_____

Tomorrow I choose:

_____

Day #94

1. What went well for you today? Give at least one example.

_____

_____

_____

2. Where is your "happy" place? Where do you go and instantly feel happy?

_____

_____

3. What frustrates you and how do you generally respond to frustrations?

_____

_____

4. How do you get yourself into a peaceful state of mind? ♡

_____

_____

_____

5. What are the 5 things that you are most grateful for today?

_____

_____

Tomorrow I choose:

_____

_____

♡ Tip: A great way to get into a peaceful state of mind is to close your eyes and visualize yourself in a place that feels calm and relaxing. This could be a magical garden, a serene sunset, or, as my son likes to visualize, a warm, sunny day at the beach. Remember to take your breaths too!

Day #95

1. What is an area in your life that you have been working on improving? What results have your seen?

_____

_____

2. How do you feel when you see yourself improving your life?

_____

_____

3. When was the last time you recall feeling discouraged? What happened?

_____

_____

_____

4. What is an improvement you can choose today that will help you deal with feeling discouraged in the future?

_____

_____

_____

5. What are the 5 things that you are most grateful for today?

_____

_____

Tomorrow I choose:

_____

Day #96

1. What was your favorite part of today?

_____

_____

2. If you could make a rule that would benefit the world, what would it be and how would it be beneficial?

_____

_____

3. When do you feel at your best? Think of who you are around, what you are doing, and where you are. Write at least 3 sentences.

_____

_____

_____

4. What challenge are you most proud of yourself for overcoming?

_____

_____

_____

5. What are the 5 things that you are most grateful for today?

_____

_____

Tomorrow I choose:

_____

Day #97

1. When you are not feeling connected to your happy heart, what tools are you using to get back into alignment?

_____

_____

2. Do you trust yourself? Explain why or why not.

_____

_____

3. Who do you feel are your top 3 allies and why? ♡

_____

_____

_____

4. If you could donate $5,000 to a specific charity or cause, where would you donate the money and why?

_____

_____

5. What are the 5 things that you are most grateful for today?

_____

_____

♡ Tip: An ally is someone who you can depend on to have your back and support you when you are in need. They are people who care about your well-being and feelings. They are on your side, and you can count on them.

Tomorrow I choose:

_____

_____

Day #98

1. What surprised you in a positive way today?

_____

_____

2. Did you stay focused on your goals today? Explain.

_____

_____

3. Reflecting upon the day, what is one moment that took you out of your happy heart and how did you handle the situation? If you stayed centered all day, recall the last time that you went out of your happy heart and share your experience.

_____

_____

4. What is your favorite thing to see in nature and how does it make you feel when you see it? ♡

_____

_____

5. What are the 5 things that you are most grateful for today?

_____

_____

Tomorrow I choose:

_____

_____

♡ Tip: Think of something in nature that, when you look at it, gives you a sense of calmness or happiness. For example, I love seeing rainbows, sunsets, beautiful flowers, butterflies, and lush forests, to name a few. Once you have selected your item, close your eyes and imagine you are having an experience in its presence.

Day #99

1. What was the biggest challenge that you faced today and how did you handle it?

_____

_____

2. Were you proud of how you handled the challenge, or would you handle it differently next time? Explain.

_____

_____

_____

3. How would you describe your attitude today? Use at least 3 adjectives.

_____

_____

_____

4. Is there anything that you could change in your attitude that will make tomorrow even more successful? Explain.

_____

_____

5. What are the 5 things that you are most grateful for today?

_____

_____

Tomorrow I choose:

_____

Day #100

1. When was the last time that you felt overwhelmed, and how did you cope with it?

_____

_____

_____

2. What is something that you learned about life today?

_____

_____

_____

3. Who do you confide in when you need someone to talk to? Include how it feels to have a confidante.

_____

_____

4. What qualities does this person have that makes you feel safe to confide in them?

_____

_____

5. What are the 5 things that you are most grateful for today?

_____

_____

Tomorrow I choose:

_____

Day #101

1. Over the past few days, when did you experience feeling appreciated? Explain what happened and how you felt.

_____

_____

_____

2. How did you express appreciation today?

_____

_____

3. What color best suits your mood today and why?

_____

_____

_____

4. What did you like best and least about today?

_____

_____

5. What are the 5 things that you are most grateful for today?

_____

_____

Tomorrow I choose:

_____

Day #102

1. How have you looked on the bright side of a difficult situation over the past month? Give details about the circumstance.

_____

_____

2. Did you speak well of others today? Explain.

_____

_____

3. What is one thing that upsets you that you realize is not beneficial to allow to get under your skin? Be descriptive with your explanation. ♡

_____

_____

4. Do you feel that you did your best today? Explain.

_____

_____

_____

5. What are the 5 things that you are most grateful for today?

_____

_____

Tomorrow I choose:

_____

♡ Tip: Often we become attached to results. We have expectations of ourselves that, when not met, cause us to feel disappointed or upset. It is important to learn to observe your thoughts and behavior. If you are having a moment where you feel triggered, try to step back and observe. Ask yourself if this is serving your best interest. Ask yourself how you can move in a direction that feels better. Try to be gentle with yourself. No one is perfect and everyone has moments like these. What we can do is learn through observation and behavior modification.

Day #103

1. Do you take the opinions of others personally? Explain. ♡

_____

_____

_____

2. How is your favorite food similar to your happy heart. Have fun with this! Explain in detail.

_____

_____

3. Were you a good friend today? Give an example of how you were or weren't.

_____

_____

4. What are 3 qualities that make someone a good friend?

1. _____

2. _____

3. _____

♡ Tip: Work on knowing who you are and knowing that you are worthy. Know that you are unique and beautifully YOU. Once you know your truth it will not matter what anyone else says. You will be able to hear constructive criticism and decide if it applies to you without feeling attacked. Learning to not take things personally is one of the greatest pathways to a happy and peaceful heart.

5. What are the 5 things that you are most grateful for today?

_____

_____

Tomorrow I choose:

_____

Day #104

1. Would you consider yourself a patient person? Explain why or why not.

_____

_____

_____

2. What are 3 adjectives that best describe your personality?

1._____   3._____

2._____

3. Do you feel alone at times? Share your thoughts.

_____

_____

_____

4. What are you most looking forward to over the next few days? ♡

_____

_____

5. What are the 5 things that you are most grateful for today?

_____

_____

Tomorrow I choose:

_____

_____

♡ Tip: Even when things aren't going your way, there is always the opportunity to look toward something more positive. In a moment of sadness or discomfort, it is healthy to acknowledge and accept your feelings and then encourage yourself to look at something that feels more optimistic.

Day #105

1. What is a question that you would love to be asked so that others could understand you better?

_____

_____

_____

2. How would you answer the question?

_____

_____

_____

3. What would you hope others would learn about you in asking that question and hearing your answer?

_____

_____

_____

4. On a scale of 1 to 10 (10 being the highest) how do you feel about yourself today and why?

_____

5. What are the 5 things that you are most grateful for today?

_____

_____

Tomorrow I choose:

_____

Day #106

1. What is one struggle that you have experienced over the past week or so?

_____

_____

2. What is one positive step that you have taken to cope with your struggle?

_____

_____

3. What is something that you can choose to do tomorrow that will have a positive impact on your life?

_____

_____

4. What are 3 acts of kindness that you have performed over the past week? ♡

_____

_____

_____

_____

5. What are the 5 things that you are most grateful for today?

_____

_____

Tomorrow I choose:

_____

♡ Tip: Acts of kindness have been shown to not only bring a sense of happiness and appreciation to the receiver but also to the giver. Research has shown that the person acting in a kind way benefits too. Some of these benefits include the strengthening of one's immune system, improved cognitive performance, increased energy, improved mood, and happiness, to name a few. Filling your heart with love and spreading kindness leads to clarity of thinking and a decrease in the stress hormone cortisol.

Day #107

1. What inspired you today? Give an example.

_____

_____

_____

2. When thinking about the funniest memory that you have, what comes to mind? Explain what happened.

_____

_____

_____

3. Did you practice compassion today? Explain why or why not.

_____

_____

_____

4. In what way would you like others to show more compassion toward you?

_____

_____

5. What are the 5 things that you are most grateful for today?

_____

_____

Tomorrow I choose:

_____

Day #108

1. Where have you seen the most improvement in your life over the past few months?

_____

_____

2. How does life feel better than it did a few months ago? Explain.

_____

_____

_____

3. How have you recently been an encouragement to your loved ones and peers? Share at least one example.

_____

_____

_____

4. What did you do today that your future self will thank you for?

_____

_____

_____

5. What are the 5 things that you are most grateful for today?

_____

_____

Tomorrow I choose:

_____

Day #109

1. What are your favorite activities to do with your friends? Name at least 3.

_____

_____

_____

2. When is the last time that you felt left out? What happened?

_____

_____

_____

3. What did you enjoy with a friend or friends today?

_____

_____

4. If you could share any experience with a friend, what would you like to do and what would make it special?

_____

_____

_____

5. What are the 5 things that you are most grateful for today?

_____

_____

Tomorrow I choose:

_____

Day #110

1. How do you feel when it is sunny outside? Use at least 3 adjectives to explain.

_____

_____

_____

2. Is your mood affected when it's gloomy outside? Explain.

_____

_____

_____

3. What did you do today that lifted your spirits?

_____

_____

4. What are 3 ways that you experienced love and/or appreciation today?

1. _____

2. _____

3. _____

5. What are the 5 things that you are most grateful for today?

_____

_____

Tomorrow I choose:

_____

Day #111

1. Do you prefer to express your feelings verbally, physically, or in writing, and why?

_____

_____

2. Did you experience life in a positive or negative way today? Share an example.

_____

_____

_____

3. What are you changing from today that will make tomorrow better?

_____

_____

_____

4. What are your most incredible qualities? Name 5.

1. I am: _____   4. I am: _____

2. I am: _____   5. I am: _____

3. I am: _____

5. What are the 5 things that you are most grateful for today?

_____

_____

Tomorrow I choose:

_____

Day #112

1. What is a question that someone could ask you that would help you share your feelings more openly?

_____

_____

2. How would you answer that question?

_____

_____

3. Touch an article of clothing that you are wearing. Use your fingers to feel the fabric. Do this for a minute or so. What does the fabric feel like? How did the feeling change as you spent more time observing your senses? How do you feel in this moment?

_____

_____

_____

4. What is something you experienced while being completely present?

_____

_____

5. What are the 5 things that you are most grateful for today?

_____

_____

Tomorrow I choose:

_____

Day #113

1. What song most reflects your life right now and why?

_____

_____

2. Who did you feel most connected with today? Explain why you felt so connected to this person.

_____

_____

_____

3. Picture yourself on a magic carpet ride. Where would you go? How do you imagine it would feel?

_____

_____

_____

4. What sound is the most soothing to your ears and why?

_____

_____

5. What are the 5 things that you are most grateful for today?

_____

_____

Tomorrow I choose:

_____

Day #114

1. What was your most optimistic thought today?

_____

_____

2. What is a past hurt that you haven't been able to let go of? Explain what happened and why you have found it difficult to release it.

_____

_____

_____

3. With the tools you are learning, what can you do today to help you to let go of your past hurt?

_____

_____

4. How does it feel when you bring happiness to others?

_____

_____

_____

5. What are the 5 things that you are most grateful for today?

_____

_____

Tomorrow I choose:

_____

Day #115

1. Were you polite today? Give an example of how you were or were not.

_____

_____

_____

2. How did you handle a difficult situation in a positive way recently?

_____

_____

_____

3. How well have you been staying in your happy heart? Give a couple of details.

_____

_____

_____

4. If you could volunteer your time for a good cause, what would you do and why?

_____

_____

5. What are the 5 things that you are most grateful for today?

_____

_____

Tomorrow I choose:

_____

Day #116

1. When was the last time that you dealt with conflict? What happened?

_____

_____

_____

_____

2. When you deal with conflict, what emotions do you generally experience?

_____

_____

3. What is one way that you could deal with conflict in a healthier way?

_____

_____

_____

4. How did you feel overall today?

_____

_____

5. What are the 5 things that you are most grateful for today?

_____

_____

Tomorrow I choose:

_____

Day #117

1. Write a sentence explaining whether or not you feel centered in your happy heart today.

_____

_____

2. If you were to use 3 adjectives to describe yourself today, what would they be and how do you feel about them?

1. _____   3. _____

2. _____

_____

_____

3. What inspired you today? Share what happened.

_____

_____

4. If you were to paint a picture of how you are feeling, what would the picture look like? Give details.

_____

_____

5. What are the 5 things that you are most grateful for today?

_____

_____

Tomorrow I choose:

_____

Day #118

1. When you are feeling sad, where do you feel the sadness located in your body?

_____

_____

2. When you are happy, where do you feel it in your body? ♡

_____

_____

3. What does it feel like when you accept your more difficult feelings into your heart? Explain.

_____

_____

_____

4. What did you do today that your future self will thank you for?

_____

_____

5. What are the 5 things that you are most grateful for today?

_____

_____

_____

Tomorrow I choose:

_____

♡ Tip: All feelings are important. When you are able to feel them and accept them, even the yucky feelings no longer control you. Remember to observe where your feelings are located in your body. Once you locate them, you can close your eyes and state your acceptance of them. As you do, visualize moving the feeling from wherever it is located into your heart. A happy heart is a heart filled with feelings that have been accepted.

Day #119

1. When was the last time that you felt appreciated? Explain.

_____

_____

_____

2. Would you prefer to hear how loved you are with words or feel it through actions? Explain.

_____

_____

_____

3. What did you prioritize today and why?

_____

_____

_____

4. On a scale of 1 to 10 (10 being the best), how was your day today? What happened?

_____

_____

5. What are the 5 things that you are most grateful for today?

_____

_____

Tomorrow I choose:

_____

Day #120

1. When was the last time you chose to forgive someone? What happened?

_____

_____

_____

2. When was the last time you were forgiven for something? What happened?

_____

_____

_____

3. What are 3 ways that you were productive today?

_____

_____

_____

4. How do you feel when you are being productive?

_____

_____

5. What are the 5 things that you are most grateful for today?

_____

_____

Tomorrow I choose:

_____

Day #121

1. What scares you the most?

_____

_____

2. What are 3 steps that you can take to overcome your fear?

1. _____

2. _____

3. _____

3. Were you honest today? Explain why or why not.

_____

_____

_____

4. What did you accept today that will help you in your future? Explain.

_____

_____

_____

5. What are the 5 things that you are most grateful for today?

_____

_____

Tomorrow I choose:

_____

Day #122

1. What are 3 positive things that you can say about one person who you have a complicated relationship with?

_____

_____

_____

2. If you were to design a birthday party for yourself and you had an unlimited budget, what would your party look like? Where would it be? Who would you invite? Give lots of details.

_____

_____

3. When did you feel your best today? Explain.

_____

_____

4. What are 5 positive qualities you exhibited today?

1. _____   4. _____

2. _____   5. _____

3. _____

5. What are the 5 things that you are most grateful for today?

_____

_____

Tomorrow I choose:

_____

Day #123

1. What needs do you have that you have not been putting first? Explain.

_____

_____

_____

2. Do you feel that you are critical of yourself? Explain why or why not.

_____

_____

_____

3. How could you improve the way that you talk to yourself?

_____

_____

4. What was your biggest obstacle today? What happened?

_____

_____

_____

5. What are the 5 things that you are most grateful for today?

_____

_____

Tomorrow I choose:

_____

Day #124

1. How has your vision for your life changed over the past few months? Give details.

_____

_____

_____

2. Did you feel empowered today? Explain how or how not.

_____

_____

_____

3. What personal strength are you most thankful for and why?

_____

_____

_____

4. Where do you go when you want to be surrounded by good energy?

_____

_____

5. What are the 5 things that you are most grateful for today?

_____

_____

Tomorrow I choose:

_____

Day #125

1. How do you generally show love? Do you use words, actions, gifts, time, etc.?

_____

_____

_____

2. How do you prefer to receive love from others? Explain.

_____

_____

3. How did you show love today? Give an example.

_____

_____

_____

4. How did you receive love today? Give an example.

_____

_____

_____

5. What are the 5 things that you are most grateful for today?

_____

_____

Tomorrow I choose:

_____

Day #126

1. What is something that you did really well today, and did it come naturally to you or did you have to work hard to make it happen?

_____

_____

_____

2. What song do you listen to that gives you an instant mood boost? What emotions do you feel when you hear it?

_____

_____

3. How could those around you make you feel more loved? Explain.

_____

_____

4. How did you show yourself love today? What happened?

_____

_____

_____

5. What are the 5 things that you are most grateful for today?

_____

_____

Tomorrow I choose:

_____

Day #127

1. Have you felt excluded by friends recently? If so, how did you feel and what happened?

_____

_____

_____

2. What type of weather best represents how you are feeling today and why?

_____

_____

3. Who is the most interesting person that you have ever met? What made them so interesting?

_____

_____

_____

4. Did you feel energized today? Why or why not? Explain.

_____

_____

_____

5. What are the 5 things that you are most grateful for today?

_____

_____

Tomorrow I choose:

_____

Day #128

1. What are 5 ways that you like to exercise and participate in physical activity?

1. _____   4. _____

2. _____   5. _____

3. _____

2. What does loving yourself feel like? Explain. If you're not quite there, how do you think it will feel once you get there?

_____

_____

3. If you found a purse or wallet with a bunch of money in it, what would you do with it? Explain your answer.

_____

_____

_____

4. What is something you're looking forward to over the next few days?

_____

_____

5. What are the 5 things that you are most grateful for today?

_____

_____

Tomorrow I choose:

_____

Day #129

1. When you hurt a friend's feelings, are you quick to apologize? Explain why or why not.

_____

_____

_____

2. When you apologize, do you generally use words or actions? Explain.

_____

_____

_____

3. Did you use your time wisely today? Explain why or why not.

_____

_____

_____

4. Who is the funniest person that you know and why?

_____

_____

5. What are the 5 things that you are most grateful for today?

_____

_____

Tomorrow I choose:

_____

Day #130

1. When was the last time that you felt disappointed? Explain what happened and how you dealt with it.

_____

_____

_____

2. If you could trade places with anyone you know for a day, who would it be and what would you do?

_____

_____

_____

3. How would your best friend describe you?

_____

_____

4. What do you do when you are in your happy heart and feeling joyful?

_____

_____

5. What are the 5 things that you are most grateful for today?

_____

_____

Tomorrow I choose:

_____

Day #131

1. How do you deal with friends when they are in in a bad mood? Explain.

_____

_____

2. If you could go on a vacation anywhere, where would you go and what would you do?

_____

_____

_____

3. What is something challenging that you have recently had to overcome? Explain.

_____

_____

_____

4. How did you feel when you overcame the challenge?

_____

_____

_____

5. What are the 5 things that you are most grateful for today?

_____

_____

Tomorrow I choose:

_____

Day #132

1. What could have made today better? Explain.

_____

_____

_____

2. What are 3 things that feel scary to you?

1. _____

2. _____

3. _____

3. How do you deal with feeling scared?

_____

_____

4. What are your 5 most prioritized values?

1. _____   4. _____

2. _____   5. _____

3. _____

5. What are the 5 things that you are most grateful for today?

_____

_____

Tomorrow I choose:

_____

Day #133

1. Do you prefer to relax by yourself or with others? Explain.

_____

_____

2. What is one compliment someone has given you that has made a lasting impact on your life, and how did hearing it make you feel?

_____

_____

_____

3. If you had to stay outside all day, what would you do?

_____

_____

_____

4. Do you feel that you were centered in your happy heart today? Why or why not?

_____

_____

_____

5. What are the 5 things that you are most grateful for today?

_____

_____

Tomorrow I choose:

_____

Day #134

1. What is one experience over the past few weeks that has impacted you in a major way? What happened and what emotions did you experience?

_____

_____

_____

2. What are 3 things you can do to turn a bad attitude around?

1. _____

2. _____

3. _____

3. How do you feel when you shift a bad attitude into a better one?

_____

_____

4. What did you experience today that will make you a better person? Explain. ♡

_____

_____

_____

5. What are the 5 things that you are most grateful for today?

_____

_____

Tomorrow I choose:

_____

♡ Tip: Any improvement or growth is awesome! Even the smallest step forward can lead to big results.

Day #135

1. Pick 3 people who mean a lot to you and list 1 thing that you can thank each of them for.

1. _____

2. _____

3. _____

2. What does it mean to you to be generous?

_____

_____

3. How do you feel when people are generous with you?

_____

_____

_____

4. Would you consider yourself to be a generous person? Why or why not?

_____

_____

_____

5. What are the 5 things that you are most grateful for today?

_____

_____

Tomorrow I choose:

_____

Day #136

1. On a scale of 1 to 10 (10 being the best), how are you feeling today? Explain your score in detail.

_____

_____

2. Use 5 words to describe your day.

1. _____   4. _____

2. _____   5. _____

3. _____

3. What is the most incredible true story you have ever heard? What made it so amazing to you?

_____

_____

4. What is the biggest decision that you have made over the past month? How did it feel to make it?

_____

_____

_____

5. What are the 5 things that you are most grateful for today?

_____

_____

Tomorrow I choose:

_____

Day #137

1. Do you feel comfortable asking for help when you need it? Explain why or why not.

_____

_____

2. In what 5 ways were you kind today?

1. _____

2. _____

3. _____

4. _____

5. _____

3. How do you feel when you are being kind?

_____

_____

4. How do you feel when you are being unkind?

_____

_____

5. What are the 5 things that you are most grateful for today?

_____

_____

Tomorrow I choose:

_____

Day #138

1. When do you feel the most secure in your life? Explain.

_____

_____

2. What is a tradition that you have and love and why? If you do not have any traditions that you love, what is one that you would like to have and why?

_____

_____

_____

3. What are 3 ways you could give back to the community?

1. _____

2. _____

3. _____

4. How do you feel when you help others?

_____

_____

_____

5. What are the 5 things that you are most grateful for today?

_____

_____

Tomorrow I choose:

_____

Day #139

1. What is one habit that you are focused on changing and why?

_____

_____

_____

2. What are your 3 most productive habits?

1. _____

2. _____

3. _____

3. What does it feel like to be around someone who acts entitled? ♡

_____

_____

_____

4. What are 5 ways that you can make sure that you do not act entitled?

1. _____

_____

♡ Tip: When you live in gratitude, you are thankful for what you have. When you are entitled, you make unrealistic demands and believe your expectations should be catered to. You are demanding as opposed to being thankful. An attitude of gratitude is always the more fruitful path.

2. _____

_____

3. _____

_____

(continued on the next page...)

Day #139, continued

4. _____

_____

5. _____

_____

5. What are the 5 things that you are most grateful for today?

_____

_____

_____

Tomorrow I choose:

_____

_____

Day #140

1. On a scale of 1 to 10 (10 being the happiest), how would you score the way you have been feeling over the past week? Explain your scoring.

_____

_____

2. If someone entrusted you with one million dollars to help the world, how would you spend it?

_____

_____

3. What are 3 things that frustrate you in life?

_____

_____

_____

4. What is a positive way that you recently handled frustration and one way that you would like to improve on how you handle feeling frustrated? Explain.

_____

_____

_____

5. What are the 5 things that you are most grateful for today?

_____

_____

Tomorrow I choose:

_____

Day #141

1. In thinking about how you deal with conflict with loved ones, what is one thing you do well and what is one thing that you could do better?

_____

_____

_____

2. What made you smile today? What happened?

_____

_____

3. What 5 of your character traits are you most proud of?

1. _____   4. _____

2. _____   5. _____

3. _____

4. How does it feel to acknowledge your character strengths?

_____

_____

5. What are the 5 things that you are most grateful for today?

_____

_____

Tomorrow I choose:

_____

Day #142

1. Do you believe that you are smart? Explain why or why not.

_____

_____

2. What 3 abilities do you have that exemplify your intelligence?

_____

_____

_____

3. What negative self-talk do you hear in your mind that holds you back? Explain.

_____

_____

_____

4. In observing your negative thoughts, can you think of 2-3 ways that you can improve your mindset? Explain.

_____

_____

_____

5. What are the 5 things that you are most grateful for today?

_____

_____

Tomorrow I choose:

_____

Day #143

1. Do you believe that you are a good person? Explain.

_____

_____

_____

2. In your opinion, what qualities and values does a good person have?

_____

_____

_____

3. What qualities or values would you like to improve upon to make yourself an even better person?

_____

_____

4. Have you ever given into peer pressure? If you have, explain what happened, and if you have not, explain how you stay true to yourself.

_____

_____

5. What are the 5 things that you are most grateful for today?

_____

_____

Tomorrow I choose:

_____

Day #144

1. On a scale of 1 to 10 (10 being the best) how good is your self-esteem right now? Explain your rating.

_____

_____

2. What are a few positive habits that you can work into your life that will help improve your self-esteem?

_____

_____

_____

3. Imagine yourself with amazing self-esteem, how would your life be different? How would you feel different than you do right now?

_____

_____

_____

4. Do you believe it is easier to be happy when you have a positive mindset? Explain.

_____

_____

5. What are the 5 things that you are most grateful for today?

_____

_____

Tomorrow I choose:

_____

Day #145

1. Are you struggling in any areas of your life? This could be in school, with friends, at home, personally, emotionally. Explain in detail.

_____

_____

_____

2. How would you like to be supported while going through your challenges? What would be beneficial to you?

_____

_____

3. Who is someone that you can reach out to for support? ♡

_____

_____

4. What is the best thing that you experienced today and why?

_____

_____

_____

5. What are the 5 things that you are most grateful for today?

_____

_____

Tomorrow I choose:

_____

♡ Tip: Being able to ask for support is a quality of a healthy mindset and strength. If you are struggling, seeking help is the best way to get back on track and back into your happiest heart.

Day #146

1. Were you encouraging to others today? Explain why or why not.

_____

_____

_____

2. Using the 5 senses below, how do you experience joy?

1. Joy feels like: _____

2. Joy tastes like: _____

3. Joy smells like: _____

4. Joy looks like: _____

5. Joy sounds like: _____

3. When was the last time you felt angry? What happened?

_____

_____

4. What are 2 ways you handle anger well, and what are 2 areas that you want to improve upon?

_____

_____

_____

_____

(continued on the next page...)

Day #146, continued

5. What are the 5 things that you are most grateful for today?

_____

_____

_____

Tomorrow I choose:

_____

_____

Day #147

1. Did you feel cheerful today? Why or why not?

_____

_____

2. Has your mood been more positive or negative over the past few days? Explain.

_____

_____

3. Do you believe that you are worthy of a wonderful life? Explain. ♡

_____

_____

_____

4. What is something that you have been working on that you hope to improve but you did not master today?

_____

_____

♡ Tip: You are absolutely worthy of an amazing life. The secret to receiving it is believing it. Remember no one is perfect. Everyone makes mistakes. Forgive yourself for anything that you are holding onto that causes you to feel guilt or shame. Look at yourself in the mirror and speak 5 things that you love about yourself every morning. Positive self-talk is essential to growing your sense of self-worth.

5. What are the 5 things that you are most grateful for today?

_____

_____

_____

Tomorrow I choose:

_____

Day #148

1. What does positivity feel like to you?

_____

_____

2. What do you like most and least about school?

_____

_____

_____

3. What is something that could have made today better? Explain.

_____

_____

_____

4. What are your 5 most positive personality traits?

1. _____   4. _____

2. _____   5. _____

3. _____

5. What are the 5 things that you are most grateful for today?

_____

_____

Tomorrow I choose:

_____

Day #149

1. Did you go to sleep with positive or negative thoughts last night, and what is the last thought you remember thinking?

_____

_____

_____

2. How can you improve your thoughts before falling asleep?

_____

_____

3. What is something that you did for someone else today? How did it make you feel?

_____

_____

4. If you were on a deserted island and could only have 5 things with you, what would you make sure to have with you?

1. _____   4. _____

2. _____   5. _____

3. _____

5. What are the 5 things that you are most grateful for today?

_____

_____

Tomorrow I choose:

_____

Day #150

1. From the time you woke up today until now, how has your mood either improved or declined? Explain.

_____

_____

2. When did you feel most at ease today? What happened?

_____

_____

_____

3. When did you feel most stressed today? What happened?

_____

_____

_____

4. What have you learned by observing all of your emotions without judgement?

_____

_____

_____

5. What are the 5 things that you are most grateful for today?

_____

_____

Tomorrow I choose:

_____

Day #151

1. When did you feel most loved today? What happened?

_____

_____

2. What are 3 positive affirmations that you can give yourself right now?

1. _____

2. _____

3. _____

3. What are 3 positive affirmations that you could give your best friend right now?

1. _____

2. _____

3. _____

4. Will you share these affirmations with your best friend? Why or why not?

_____

_____

_____

5. What are the 5 things that you are most grateful for today?

_____

_____

Tomorrow I choose:

_____

Day #152

1. What is one way that you prioritized your well-being today?

_____

_____

2. How did it feel to put yourself first?

_____

_____

_____

3. How do you feel when you receive constructive feedback? Explain.

_____

_____

_____

4. Do you feel that you did your best today? Explain.

_____

_____

_____

5. What are the 5 things that you are most grateful for today?

_____

_____

Tomorrow I choose:

_____

Day #153

1. Close your eyes and visualize something that makes you feel warm and happy. Describe what you see in detail.

_____

_____

_____

2. What is one thing that surprised you in a positive way today?

_____

_____

_____

3. How do you feel when you are pleasantly surprised? Explain.

_____

_____

_____

4. If you could be a teacher in any subject, what would you teach and why?

_____

_____

5. What are the 5 things that you are most grateful for today?

_____

_____

Tomorrow I choose:

_____

Day #154

1. On a scale of 1 to 10 (10 being the best), how did you feel when you woke up today? Describe your score using at least 3 adjectives.

_____

_____

_____

2. What is one word of encouragement that you need to hear today?

_____

_____

3. What proactive step(s) did you take today to improve your day?

_____

_____

_____

4. What physical activity do you enjoy doing the most? How do you feel when you are doing it?

_____

_____

5. What are the 5 things that you are most grateful for today?

_____

_____

Tomorrow I choose:

_____

Day #155

1. What is something that you are currently struggling with?

_____

_____

_____

2. Do you feel that you have support right now? Explain why or why not.

_____

_____

_____

3. What is one positive step forward that you took today and how did it feel?

_____

_____

_____

4. If you could have any superpower for the day, what would it be and what would you do?

_____

_____

5. What are the 5 things that you are most grateful for today?

_____

_____

Tomorrow I choose:

_____

Day #156

1. Do you find it challenging to express your feelings? Explain.

_____

_____

_____

2. What makes your body feel calm and relaxed?

_____

_____

3. What are 3 blessings in your life?

1. _____

2. _____

3. _____

4. What is one thing you are looking forward to tomorrow and why?

_____

_____

_____

5. What are the 5 things that you are most grateful for today?

_____

_____

Tomorrow I choose:

_____

Day #157

1. What inspired you today? Explain.

_____

_____

_____

2. What do you like to do when you are feeling really happy? Give details.

_____

_____

3. What is one way that you have been hard on yourself, and how can you be gentler with yourself?

_____

_____

_____

4. What are 2 things that made you smile today and why?

_____

_____

_____

5. What are the 5 things that you are most grateful for today?

_____

_____

Tomorrow I choose:

_____

Day #158

1. Did you live in gratitude today? Explain.

_____

_____

_____

2. How did you choose to stay positive today? Explain.

_____

_____

_____

3. What makes you an awesome friend?

_____

_____

4. If you could go back in time, fast forward to the future, or stay in the present, what would you choose and why? Give details.

_____

_____

_____

5. What are the 5 things that you are most grateful for today?

_____

_____

Tomorrow I choose:

_____

Day #159

1. What improvements have you seen in the way that you think over the past month or so? Explain.

_____

_____

_____

2. Did you feel appreciated today? Explain why or why not.

_____

_____

3. How is being organized an asset in life? Explain.

_____

_____

4. If you were a parent and your child lied to you, how would you discipline them? Explain.

_____

_____

_____

5. What are the 5 things that you are most grateful for today?

_____

_____

Tomorrow I choose:

_____

Day #160

1. Is there anything that you would like an apology for from someone close to you? Explain.

_____

_____

_____

2. Is there anything that you need to apologize for? Explain.

_____

_____

3. What is the most positive thing that happened today, and how did it make you feel?

_____

_____

4. Over the past few days what was your happiest moment and how did it feel? Give details.

_____

_____

_____

5. What are the 5 things that you are most grateful for today?

_____

_____

Tomorrow I choose:

_____

Day #161

1. What is the hardest rule for you to follow? Explain.

_____

_____

_____

2. Who is the most supportive person in your life, and how will they help you reach your goals?

_____

_____

_____

3. What is one way that you choose to stay positive today? Give details.

_____

_____

4. What are 3 compliments you can give yourself today?

1. _____

2. _____

3. _____

5. What are the 5 things that you are most grateful for today?

_____

_____

Tomorrow I choose:

_____

Day #162

1. What inspires you to be your best? Explain.

_____

_____

_____

2. Do you feel confident in yourself? Explain your observations.

_____

_____

_____

3. What is your favorite subject to learn about in school and why?

_____

_____

4. What is the kindest thing someone did for you over the past few days? How did it make you feel?

_____

_____

_____

5. What are the 5 things that you are most grateful for today?

_____

_____

Tomorrow I choose:

_____

Day #163

1. Do you feel that you did your best today? Explain why or why not.

_____

_____

_____

2. What are 3 short term goals that you are committed to accomplishing?

1. _____

2. _____

3. _____

3. If you could help one person today, who would it be and how would you help them?

_____

_____

_____

4. Who would you like to spend more quality time with and why?

_____

_____

5. What are the 5 things that you are most grateful for today?

_____

_____

Tomorrow I choose:

_____

Day #164

1. What are 5 positive things that happened today?

1. _____

2. _____

3. _____

4. _____

5. _____

2. What would your ideal day look like and how do you imagine it would feel? Be descriptive.

_____

_____

3. Did you feel upset at any point today? If so, what happened? If not, how did it feel to have a consistently good day?

_____

_____

4. When you feel upset, how do you cope with your feelings?

_____

5. What are the 5 things that you are most grateful for today?

_____

_____

Tomorrow I choose:

_____

Day #165

1. Did you make the most of today? Give details.

_____

_____

_____

2. How did you practice acceptance today?

_____

_____

_____

3. Take a moment to be silent. Listen to the sounds around you. What sound did you hear and what feelings did it evoke?

_____

_____

_____

4. What is a lesson that you learned today?

_____

_____

5. What are the 5 things that you are most grateful for today?

_____

_____

Tomorrow I choose:

_____

Day #166

1. What taste brings you the most joy? Explain in detail, using at least 5 adjectives.

_____

_____

_____

2. If you could touch kindness, what would it feel like?

_____

_____

3. How did you follow through on your commitments today?

_____

_____

_____

4. What does it feel like to be productive?

_____

_____

_____

5. What are the 5 things that you are most grateful for today?

_____

_____

Tomorrow I choose:

_____

Day #167

1. Did you feel loved today? Explain what happened and why you either did or did not feel loved.

_____

_____

2. If you could have a conversation with anyone in the world, who would it be and what would you talk about? Write at least 5 sentences.

_____

_____

_____

_____

_____

3. What did you do today that brought you closer to your happy heart?

_____

4. How did you keep an open mind today?

_____

_____

5. What are the 5 things that you are most grateful for today?

_____

_____

Tomorrow I choose:

_____

Day #168

1. When do you find that your mind starts to race the most? Give details.

_____

_____

2. What do you do to relieve your mind when it is overthinking?

_____

3. On a scale of 1 to 10 (10 being the most), how much anxiety do you generally feel, and what coping mechanisms do you turn to when you are feeling anxious?

_____

_____

_____

4. What are 3 new positive habits that can help you calm your mind and reduce any anxiety that you might have? ♡

_____

_____

_____

5. What are the 5 things that you are most grateful for today?

_____

_____

Tomorrow I choose:

_____

♡ Tip: Anxiety stems from thinking about the future, which is unknown. So in the moments where you feel anxious and your mind seems to be spinning out of control, you can use breathing techniques as well as the following grounding technique to help bring you back to the present moment. Put your hands in water. Start with warm water. Notice how your hands feel front and back as well as on your palms. Next do the same with cold water. Compare and contrast how the different temperatures feel. If you are at school when the anxiety comes on, you can wash your hands in the bathroom with one temperature and pay attention to the way the water feels as you wash your hands. Remember you cannot control what goes on around you, but you can learn to control what goes on inside of you. It takes awareness and practice, but you can do it!

Day #169

1. What is the most joyful thought that came to your mind today?

_____

_____

2. How did that joyful thought feel?

_____

_____

_____

3. What was the most distressing thought that came to mind today?

_____

_____

_____

4. How did feeling that distressed thought feel?

_____

_____

_____

5. What are the 5 things that you are most grateful for today?

_____

_____

Tomorrow I choose:

_____

Day #170

1. What made you stop and appreciate your life today?

_____

_____

_____

2. How does it feel to slow down and appreciate your life?

_____

_____

3. Where have you seen the greatest improvement in your life over the past few months?

_____

_____

_____

4. What is your favorite extracurricular activity and why?

_____

_____

_____

5. What are the 5 things that you are most grateful for today?

_____

_____

Tomorrow I choose:

_____

Day #171

1. When you feel lonely, what do you do to help yourself? Give examples.

_____

_____

2. What is one way that you can improve your mindset before going to bed tonight?

_____

_____

3. What is something that you are currently doing that you are passionate about? Explain.

_____

_____

_____

4. If you could relive one day all over again but change the outcome, what day would it be? Explain what happened and what you would change.

_____

_____

_____

5. What are the 5 things that you are most grateful for today?

_____

_____

Tomorrow I choose:

_____

Day #172

1. What uplifted your spirits today?

_____

_____

_____

2. Did you communicate well today? Explain.

_____

_____

3. What did you accomplish today and how did it feel?

_____

_____

_____

4. What could have made today better?

_____

_____

_____

5. What are the 5 things that you are most grateful for today?

_____

_____

Tomorrow I choose:

_____

Day #173

1. What made you feel optimistic today?

_____

_____

2. What is the value of being optimistic in life? Explain your thoughts.

_____

_____

_____

3. Did you overcome anything challenging today? What happened?

_____

_____

_____

4. If you could spend the day with one person in your life, who would it be, what would you do, and why would you want to spend the day with this person?

_____

_____

_____

5. What are the 5 things that you are most grateful for today?

_____

_____

Tomorrow I choose:

_____

Day #174

1. What is the last compliment that you received, and how did it feel to hear it?

_____

_____

2. What are you looking most forward to in the short term and what are you looking most forward to in the long term? ♡

_____

_____

_____

3. What one of your unique qualities is your favorite and why?

_____

_____

_____

4. What one of your unique qualities do you have a hard time accepting and why?

_____

_____

5. What are the 5 things that you are most grateful for today?

_____

_____

Tomorrow I choose:

_____

_____

♡ Tip: What you are able to see, you are better able to receive. When you can visualize your goals, you create momentum toward them. Keep believing in all of your goals!

Day #175

1. What in nature do you enjoy, and how does being around it make you feel?

_____

_____

_____

2. How did you help a loved one today?

_____

_____

_____

3. How did it feel to do something helpful for someone who you love?

_____

_____

4. If you could have a conversation with anyone in the world, who would you talk to and what would you want to discuss?

_____

_____

_____

5. What are the 5 things that you are most grateful for today?

_____

_____

Tomorrow I choose:

_____

Day #176

1. When you get older, do you see yourself as a business owner/boss or as an employee? Explain your thoughts.

_____

_____

2. What profession do you see yourself in when you are older, and what excites you about it?

_____

_____

_____

3. Why do you think some people bully others?

_____

_____

4. If you saw someone being bullied, what would you do? Explain.

_____

_____

5. What are the 5 things that you are most grateful for today?

_____

_____

_____

Tomorrow I choose:

_____

Day #177

1. Do you believe it is important to speak up when you are witnessing injustice? Explain.

_____

_____

_____

2. Who is a person that you have never met but who has inspired you? What makes them so inspiring?

_____

_____

_____

3. Using your 5 senses, what does inspiration:

1. Feel like: _____

2. Taste like: _____

3. Look like: _____

4. Sound like: _____

5. Smell like: _____

4. Do you believe that telling the truth is always the right thing, even if it hurts someone's feelings? Explain why or why not.

_____

_____

_____

(continued on the next page...)

Day #177, continued

5. What are the 5 things that you are most grateful for today?

_____

_____

_____

Tomorrow I choose:

_____

_____

Day #178

1. How would you describe your attitude today? Use at least 3 adjectives to describe.

_____

_____

2. If you could read the mind of anyone in your life, who would you choose and why would you want to know their every thought?

_____

_____

_____

3. Did you listen well to others today? Explain why or why not.

_____

_____

4. Do you find that you generally listen to respond or listen to hear what the other person is saying? Explain.

_____

_____

_____

5. What are the 5 things that you are most grateful for today?

_____

_____

Tomorrow I choose:

_____

Day #179

1. Have you ever lost your temper? If so, what happened and what triggered you?

_____

_____

_____

2. What are a few ways that you can maintain your composure better in the future?

_____

_____

_____

3. What do you commit to today that will better you tomorrow?

_____

_____

4. If you could create a rule that everyone in the world had to follow, what would it be and how do you believe it would benefit the world?

_____

_____

_____

5. What are the 5 things that you are most grateful for today?

_____

_____

Tomorrow I choose:

_____

Day #180

1. Who in your life stood out today and why? Give details of what happened.

_____

_____

2. How did you express your feelings in a healthy way today?

_____

_____

_____

3. On a scale of 1 to 10 (10 being the best), how would you describe your self-esteem? Explain your scoring.

_____

_____

4. What are you doing regularly to improve your self-esteem? ♡

_____

_____

5. What are the 5 things that you are most grateful for today?

_____

♡ Tip: Consistency is the key to creating any kind of lasting change. What you do to benefit your life today will absolutely help you tomorrow. Little steps taken consistently result in big and meaningful results. Trust the process! One step in the right direction can change the course of your life!

_____

Tomorrow I choose:

_____

_____

Day #181

1. What was the most fun that you had today? Explain.

_____

_____

_____

2. What emotions do you experience when you are having fun? Explain.

_____

_____

_____

3. How did you demonstrate independence today?

_____

_____

_____

4. What does being independent feel like to you?

_____

_____

5. What are the 5 things that you are most grateful for today?

_____

_____

Tomorrow I choose:

_____

Day #182

1.What are 3 moments from over the past few days where you felt your best?

1. _____

2. _____

3. _____

2. What is something that you are currently having a tough time with? Be descriptive.

_____

_____

_____

3. What are a couple of positive ways that you have been coping with this difficulty?

_____

_____

_____

4. Have you been able to accept your feelings into your heart during this time? Explain why or why not.

_____

_____

5. What are the 5 things that you are most grateful for today?

_____

_____

Tomorrow I choose:

_____

Day #183

1. What is one way that you improved as a person today? Explain.

_____

_____

2. How does it feel to acknowledge your improvements? Use at least 3 adjectives to explain your feelings.

_____

_____

_____

3. What is something that you are currently working on improving in your life, and how are you doing with it?

_____

_____

4. Over the past few days, when did you receive kindness from someone else, and how did you feel?

_____

_____

_____

5. What are the 5 things that you are most grateful for today?

_____

_____

Tomorrow I choose:

_____

Day #184

1. When do you feel safest to express yourself? Explain.

_____

_____

2. What was the most enjoyable part of your day, and how did it feel?

_____

_____

3. If you could have dinner with 3 people that you have never met, living or dead, who would they be and why?

_____

_____

_____

_____

4. What does it feel like to be encouraged? Explain.

_____

_____

_____

5. What are the 5 things that you are most grateful for today?

_____

_____

Tomorrow I choose:

_____

Day #185

1. How do you cope with stress?

_____

_____

2. Do you feel that your coping mechanisms are effective in decreasing your stress? Explain why or why not.

_____

_____

_____

3. What is something new that you would like to learn about and why?

_____

_____

4. Would you rather spend time alone doing something that you enjoy, or would you prefer to do something that you enjoy with a friend? Explain.

_____

_____

_____

5. What are the 5 things that you are most grateful for today?

_____

_____

Tomorrow I choose:

_____

Day #186

1. What was your biggest challenge today and how did you manage it in a healthy way?

_____

_____

_____

2. What could you have done to manage your challenge even better?

_____

_____

_____

3. Would you consider yourself to be polite? Explain why or why not.

_____

_____

4. Do you feel it is important to be polite? Explain your thoughts.

_____

_____

_____

5. What are the 5 things that you are most grateful for today?

_____

_____

Tomorrow I choose:

_____

Day #187

1. What is something that you can do today to move in a direction that feels good to you? Explain.

_____

_____

_____

2. What are 3 areas in your life that you are committed to improving?

1. _____

2. _____

3. _____

3. If you were to create a movie about your life, what would it be called and what genre would it be?

_____

_____

4. What dessert best describes your personality and why?

_____

_____

5. What are the 5 things that you are most grateful for today?

_____

_____

Tomorrow I choose:

_____

Day #188

1. Who do you feel that you can count on in your life and why?

_____

_____

_____

2. Do you consider yourself to be dependable? Explain why or why not?

_____

_____

3. What conversation this week has been the most meaningful to you and why?

_____

_____

_____

4. If you could be invisible for the day, what would you do and how do you imagine it would feel?

_____

_____

_____

5. What are the 5 things that you are most grateful for today?

_____

_____

Tomorrow I choose:

_____

Day #189

1. What was one good decision that you made today, and how did it feel to make it?

_____

_____

_____

2. What is one decision that you would like to have made differently today? Explain.

_____

_____

_____

3. Do you believe that next time you will choose the better way? Why or why not?

_____

_____

_____

4. Who is the most encouraging person in your life and why?

_____

_____

5. What are the 5 things that you are most grateful for today?

_____

_____

Tomorrow I choose:

_____

Day #190

1. What are you most proud of today?

_____

_____

2. If you could design a best friend, what personality and character traits would they have?

_____

_____

3. What day from the past month would you want to relive and why? Explain what happened and why you would want to relive it in detail.

_____

_____

_____

4. If you could give $1,000 to someone in need, who would you want to support and why?

_____

_____

_____

5. What are the 5 things that you are most grateful for today?

_____

_____

Tomorrow I choose:

_____

Day #191

1. What are you looking most forward to experiencing as an adult and why?

_____

_____

_____

2. Would you like to stay the age you are for an extra year? Explain why or why not?

_____

_____

_____

3. How did you overcome adversity today? Share your experience.

_____

_____

_____

4. Do you believe that adversity helps you grow? Why or why not.

_____

_____

5. What are the 5 things that you are most grateful for today?

_____

_____

Tomorrow I choose:

_____

Day #192

1. When did you feel most empowered today?

_____

_____

2. What does feeling empowered feel like to you?

_____

_____

3. What is your greatest gift to the world? Explain in detail.

_____

_____

_____

4. How does it feel knowing that you have a gift that can impact the lives of others? Express your feelings with at least 3 sentences.

_____

_____

_____

_____

5. What are the 5 things that you are most grateful for today?

_____

_____

Tomorrow I choose:

_____

Day #193

1. What is one way that you have felt inspired recently?

_____

_____

_____

2. In what ways do you believe that you are inspiring to others? Explain.

_____

_____

_____

3. How did you spread kindness today?

_____

_____

_____

4. How do you feel when you choose to be kind?

_____

_____

5. What are the 5 things that you are most grateful for today?

_____

_____

Tomorrow I choose:

_____

Day #194

1. If you could ask your 5-year-old self a question, what would you ask?

_____

_____

2. How do you think your 5-year-old self would respond?

_____

_____

_____

3. Does this response surprise you? Why or why not.

_____

_____

_____

4. In connecting with your 5-year-old self, do you feel happy or sad? Explain.

_____

_____

_____

5. What are the 5 things that you are most grateful for today?

_____

_____

Tomorrow I choose:

_____

Day #195

1. If you could ask your 30-year-old self a question, what would you ask?

_____

_____

2. Pretend that you are your 30-year-old self, how do you think you would respond?

_____

_____

_____

3. In thinking of your response, what surprised you or what did you learn?

_____

_____

_____

4. How does it feel to imagine your 30-year-old self? Use at least 3 adjectives to describe your feelings.

_____

_____

_____

5. What are the 5 things that you are most grateful for today?

_____

_____

Tomorrow I choose:

_____

Day #196

1. How were you aware of your feelings today, and were you able to understand why you felt the way you were feeling?

_____

_____

2. Do you feel that you understand yourself? Why or why not?

_____

_____

3. Do you feel understood by others? Explain.

_____

_____

4. How do you feel when you don't feel understood by others? Use at least 3 adjectives to describe your feelings.

_____

_____

_____

5. What are the 5 things that you are most grateful for today?

_____

_____

Tomorrow I choose:

_____

Day #197

1. How were you able to see things from someone else's perspective today? Explain what happened.

_____

_____

2. How did it feel to see something from a perspective different than your own?

_____

_____

3. Are you able to agree to disagree with people, or do you generally feel a need to be right? Explain.

_____

_____

_____

4. If you could be incredibly talented at something, what would it be and how do you imagine it would feel?

_____

_____

5. What are the 5 things that you are most grateful for today?

_____

_____

Tomorrow I choose:

_____

Day #198

1. How was your mood today on a scale of 1 to 10 (10 being the best)? Explain your scoring.

_____

_____

2. How do you believe that your mood impacts others. Give details.

_____

_____

_____

3. How would you rate your effort level today from 1 to 10 (10 being the best) and why?

_____

_____

_____

4. How could you improve your effort tomorrow?

_____

_____

_____

5. What are the 5 things that you are most grateful for today?

_____

_____

Tomorrow I choose:

_____

Day #199

1. Do you believe that you exceeded your goals over the past month? Explain why or why not.

_____

_____

2. If you surpassed your goals; how does it feel to exceed your expectations? If you believe that you under-achieved, how does that feel to you?

_____

_____

3. When is the last time that you recall missing the mark with something that you set out to accomplish? Explain. ♡

_____

_____

4. What are a few ways that you can get back on track when you have lost momentum with your goals? Explain.

_____

_____

5. What are the 5 things that you are most grateful for today?

_____

_____

Tomorrow I choose:

_____

_____

♡ Tip: Don't be hard on yourself. As long as you are putting in the effort, keep going. Don't worry about missing a deadline. You only fail if you give up.

Day #200

1. What did you learn today that will better your life?

_____

_____

_____

2. Do you find it easy to ask for help? Explain why or why not.

_____

_____

3. When did you feel most understood over the past few days? Explain.

_____

_____

_____

4. How do you feel when you are understood by others? Explain.

_____

_____

_____

5. What are the 5 things that you are most grateful for today?

_____

_____

Tomorrow I choose:

_____

Day #201

1. If you could give your younger self one piece of advice, what would it be?

_____

_____

_____

2. How do you think that piece of advice would have benefited you in your life today? Explain.

_____

_____

_____

3. What positive habit did you observe in yourself today? ♡

_____

_____

4. How does it feel to observe yourself gaining more positive habits?

_____

_____

5. What are the 5 things that you are most grateful for today?

_____

_____

Tomorrow I choose:

_____

_____

♡ Tip: Research has shown that it takes about 66 days before a new habit becomes automatic. The key is to be consistent in your pursuit of a more positive life, with lots of repetition.

Day #202

1. Did you demonstrate leadership today? Explain.

_____

_____

_____

2. Does leadership come naturally to you? Why or why not?

_____

_____

_____

3. When did you feel at your best today?

_____

_____

4. What has been your greatest accomplishment over the last month?

_____

_____

_____

5. What are the 5 things that you are most grateful for today?

_____

_____

Tomorrow I choose:

_____

Day #203

1. Have you ever lost a good friend? What happened?

_____

_____

_____

2. How do you believe that you could restore a relationship with this person?

_____

_____

_____

3. What was your happiest moment today? What happened?

_____

_____

4. What 5 adjectives describe your heart today?

1. _____   4. _____

2. _____   5. _____

3. _____

5. What are the 5 things that you are most grateful for today?

_____

_____

Tomorrow I choose:

_____

Day #204

1. Do you consider yourself a winner? Why or why not?

_____

_____

2. What does being a winner mean to you?

_____

_____

_____

3. If you could receive an award for something that you have done or are doing, what would it be and why would you be honored?

_____

_____

_____

4. How would you feel to receive this award?

_____

_____

_____

5. What are the 5 things that you are most grateful for today?

_____

_____

Tomorrow I choose:

_____

Day #205

1. Who is your biggest inspiration and why?

_____

_____

2. What does being inspired feel like? Explain

_____

_____

_____

3. What was the best part of today and why?

_____

_____

_____

4. How did you exhibit kindness today? ♡

_____

_____

5. What are the 5 things that you are most grateful for today?

_____

_____

Tomorrow I choose:

_____

_____

♡ Tip: Random or planned acts of kindness don't just uplift the person on the receiving end but also create a sense of well-being for the giver.

Day #206

1. If you could go back in time, would you change anything that has happened in your life? Explain why or why not?

_____

_____

2. What is one way that you chose to look at the positive today even when there was an equal opportunity to look at the negative? Explain.

_____

_____

_____

3. How do you feel when you choose to look for the positive in a situation?

_____

_____

4. Do you find it difficult to look on the bright and positive side of things? Explain why or why not.

_____

_____

_____

5. What are the 5 things that you are most grateful for today?

_____

_____

Tomorrow I choose:

_____

Day #207

1. What brought you joy today? Explain.

_____

_____

_____

2. Did you struggle at any point today finding joy? Explain why or why not.

_____

_____

_____

3. What do you feel like when you are joyful?

1. I feel: _____   4. I feel: _____

2. I feel: _____   5. I feel: _____

3. I feel: _____

4. What is one way that you could have been more efficient today?

_____

_____

5. What are the 5 things that you are most grateful for today?

_____

_____

Tomorrow I choose:

_____

Day #208

1. Were you able to stay connected to your happy heart today? If so, explain what you did to do so. If not, explain what you believe happened.

_____

_____

_____

2. What is the difference between being in your happy heart and being outside of it? Explain the difference in how you feel.

_____

_____

_____

3. What made you laugh today? How did it feel to laugh?

_____

_____

4. What is the most enjoyable thing that you did this week?

_____

_____

5. What are the 5 things that you are most grateful for today?

_____

_____

Tomorrow I choose:

_____

Day #209

1. How did you practice honesty today?

_____

_____

_____

2. Using your 5 senses and your imagination, what does being honest:

1. Feel like: _____

2. Taste like: _____

3. Look like: _____

4. Sound like: _____

5. Smell like: _____

3. What is one thing that you have been dishonest about that you are still holding onto? Explain.

_____

_____

_____

4. What, in your opinion, would be a good way to let this untruth go? Explain.

_____

_____

_____

(continued on the next page...)

Day #209, continued

5. What are the 5 things that you are most grateful for today?

_____

_____

_____

Tomorrow I choose:

_____

_____

Day #210

1. How did you step outside of your comfort zone today? Explain.

_____

_____

2. What emotions did you experience while stepping outside of your comfort zone? Explain.

_____

_____

_____

3. How can you challenge yourself to step even more out of your comfort zone tomorrow? ♡

_____

_____

4. When did you feel most encouraged today? Explain.

_____

_____

5. What are the 5 things that you are most grateful for today?

_____

_____

Tomorrow I choose:

_____

_____

♡ Tip: Stepping out of your comfort zone is what leads you to the next, better version of yourself. Walk by faith and not in fear.

Day #211

1. Share one situation where you were mindful and able to observe your thoughts today.

_____

_____

_____

2. How could you have been more mindful today?

_____

_____

3. Do you feel calmer when you are being mindful? Explain.

_____

_____

_____

4. What did you achieve today that you are most proud of?

_____

_____

_____

5. What are the 5 things that you are most grateful for today?

_____

_____

Tomorrow I choose:

_____

Day #212

1. How do you communicate your needs and preferences?

_____

_____

2. What feelings come up for you when you are communicating your needs and/or preferences? Explain.

_____

_____

_____

3. Is there someone who you need to communicate a need or preference with who you have been avoiding? Give details.

_____

_____

4. When did you feel your best today? What happened?

_____

_____

_____

5. What are the 5 things that you are most grateful for today?

_____

_____

Tomorrow I choose:

_____

Day #213

1. Who in your life does your energy increase around, and who does it decrease around? ♡

_____

_____

2. In thinking about who your energy increases around, what are their personality and behavioral traits?

_____

_____

3. In thinking about who your energy decreases around, what are their personality and behavioral traits?

_____

_____

_____

4. In considering these people and how they affect your energy, what do you realize?

_____

_____

5. What are the 5 things that you are most grateful for today?

_____

♡ Tip: Choose to spend more time with those who increase your energy and less time with people who decrease your energy. Every time you subtract a negative you leave room for more positive.

Tomorrow I choose:

_____

_____

Day #214

1. What school or family rule would you most like to change and why?

_____

_____

_____

2. What benefits do you believe would come from changing this rule?

_____

_____

_____

3. If you could invent something to help others, what would you create and why? Give details.

_____

_____

_____

4. Were you kind today? Explain.

_____

_____

5. What are the 5 things that you are most grateful for today?

_____

_____

Tomorrow I choose:

_____

Day #215

1. When you are in your happy heart, how do you feel?

1. I feel: _____

2. I feel: _____

3. I feel: _____

4. I feel: _____

5. I feel: _____

2. When you are not in your happy heart, how do you feel?

1. I feel: _____

2. I feel: _____

3. I feel: _____

4. I feel: _____

5. I feel: _____

3. What is one technique that you have used to get back into your happy heart when you are not in it? Give details.

_____

_____

_____

_____

_____

(continued on the next page...)

Day #215, continued

4. Who in your life has had the biggest impact on you this week? Explain what happened.

_____

_____

_____

_____

5. What are the 5 things that you are most grateful for today?

_____

_____

_____

Tomorrow I choose:

_____

_____

Day #216

1. What is a special talent that you have?

_____

_____

2. What does it feel like when you are spending time working on your special talent?

_____

_____

_____

3. What is an asset that you recognized about yourself today? Explain.

_____

_____

_____

4. How does it feel to recognize strengths you never knew you had?

_____

_____

_____

5. What are the 5 things that you are most grateful for today?

_____

_____

Tomorrow I choose:

_____

Day #217

1. Do you currently have any conflicts that you are dealing with? Explain either a current conflict or a past conflict that you have had to deal with.

_____

_____

_____

2. How do you generally reconcile differences with others?

_____

_____

3. Do you find your coping skills when in conflict with others effective? Explain.

_____

_____

4. In observing how you deal with conflict, what is something that you could do to improve? How would this benefit you and the situation? Explain.

_____

_____

_____

5. What are the 5 things that you are most grateful for today?

_____

_____

Tomorrow I choose:

_____

Day #218

1. What did you do for fun today?

_____

_____

2. How does it feel to be carefree and having fun? Explain using at least 3 adjectives.

_____

_____

_____

3. Are you able to stay in the present moment when you are having fun or does your mind start racing? Explain.

_____

_____

_____

4. When you aren't happy, are you able to stay present or does your mind race? Explain.

_____

_____

_____

5. What are the 5 things that you are most grateful for today?

_____

_____

Tomorrow I choose:

_____

Day #219

1. How did you motivate yourself today?

_____

_____

2. Using your 5 senses how do you experience motivation?

1. Motivation feels like: _____

2. Motivation tastes like: _____

3. Motivation smells like: _____

4. Motivation sounds like: _____

5. Motivation looks like: _____

3. Do you believe that you a motivator to others? Explain why or why not?

_____

_____

4. How will you use self-motivation to accomplish your short-term goals?

_____

_____

5. What are the 5 things that you are most grateful for today?

_____

_____

Tomorrow I choose:

_____

Day #220

1. How did you exhibit discipline today?

_____

_____

2. What does it feel like to be disciplined? Explain.

_____

_____

_____

3. In what areas of your life could you be more disciplined? Explain.

_____

_____

_____

4. Who in your life is the best example of discipline? Explain what their demonstration of discipline has taught you.

_____

_____

_____

5. What are the 5 things that you are most grateful for today?

_____

_____

Tomorrow I choose:

_____

Day #221

1. Can you tell when others aren't happy with you? If so, how can you tell? If not, why do you think you struggle to read how others feel?

_____

_____

2. How do you respond or react when people are not happy with you? ♡

_____

_____

3. Who in your life do you believe understands you and your feelings best? Explain.

_____

_____

4. How does it feel when someone "gets you"? If you have never felt understood, explain how that feels.

_____

_____

5. What are the 5 things that you are most grateful for today?

_____

_____

Tomorrow I choose:

_____

_____

♡ Tip: It is important to understand that everyone has their own thoughts, feelings, and perspectives. It is healthy to have open communication with friends and loved ones, not only to share affirmations but also to share hurts and disappointments. The key is to not take it personally when another expresses their displeasure. Instead, see it as an opportunity to grow with that person by listening with empathy and a desire to understand. Being empathetic and understanding does not mean agreeing. It simply means that you respect the other person and care about their personal experience while honoring your own.

Day #222

1. Do you feel that you are able to build solid friendships? Explain why or why not.

_____

_____

2. What does a solid friendship consist of? Explain.

_____

_____

_____

3. Who is a solid friend of yours and what qualities make them such a good friend?

_____

_____

_____

4. Who did you spend enjoyable quality time with today, and what did you do?

_____

_____

_____

5. What are the 5 things that you are most grateful for today?

_____

_____

Tomorrow I choose:

_____

Day #223

1. Look around you right now, what is something that you notice that you appreciate. Explain.

_____

2. List 5 positive affirmations about yourself:

1. _____

2. _____

3. _____

4. _____

5. _____

3. How does it feel when you state positive affirmations about yourself?

_____

4. Are you able to consciously alter your mood or mindset? If so, how do you do it? If not, how do you believe you would benefit from being able to consciously shift your mood or mindset? ♡

_____

_____

5. What are the 5 things that you are most grateful for today?

_____

_____

Tomorrow I choose:

_____

♡ Tip: Being connected to your feelings allows for you to acknowledge when you are out of your happy heart center. When you are able to identify this and know how to pick better feeling thoughts, you will be able to shift your mood or mindset all by yourself! It is important to remember that nothing outside of you is responsible for making you happy. You get to make it happen for yourself!

Day #224

1. What is the one thing that can make you smile from the inside out even on the not as good days?

_____

_____

_____

2. Was today a good day or not so good day? Explain.

_____

_____

3. What is the best advice that you ever received?

_____

_____

_____

4. How has that advice impacted your life? Explain.

_____

_____

_____

5. What are the 5 things that you are most grateful for today?

_____

_____

Tomorrow I choose:

_____

Day #225

1. What were 3 of your happiest moments that you experienced today?

1. _____

2. _____

3. _____

2. What was a moment where you can recall feeling sad today? What was happening? ♡

_____

_____

3. What made you laugh today?

_____

_____

4. How do you feel when you laugh? Explain.

_____

_____

_____

5. What are the 5 things that you are most grateful for today?

_____

_____

Tomorrow I choose:

_____

_____

♡ Tip: There are no "bad" feelings. The goal is to accept how you are feeling without judgement in your heart. To be able to identify sadness and accept it in your heart is wonderful! Close your eyes and visualize whatever sadness you are feeling being accepted with love and compassion into your heart.

Day #226

1. Who inspired you today and why?

_____

_____

2. How were you an inspiration today, and how do you believe it impacted others?

_____

_____

_____

3. How does it feel to be inspired?

_____

_____

_____

4. What are you most looking forward to tomorrow?

_____

_____

_____

5. What are the 5 things that you are most grateful for today?

_____

_____

Tomorrow I choose:

_____

Day #227

1. When was the most recent time that you were able to be positive despite being in a challenging situation? Explain.

_____

_____

_____

2. Do you feel empowered when you are able to be positive despite challenges? Explain.

_____

_____

_____

3. Were you mindful of your attitude today? Explain.

_____

_____

4. How can you improve your mindset tomorrow? Explain.

_____

_____

_____

5. What are the 5 things that you are most grateful for today?

_____

_____

Tomorrow I choose:

_____

Day #228

1. On a scale of 1 to 10 (10 being the most), how at peace did you feel today? Explain your scoring.

_____

_____

2. When does your heart feel peaceful? Explain.

_____

_____

3. Using your 5 senses, share your experience of peace.

1. Peace feels like: _____

2. Peace tastes like: _____

3. Peace smells like: _____

4. Peace looks like: _____

5. Peace sounds like: _____

4. How were you inspired today? Explain.

_____

_____

5. What are the 5 things that you are most grateful for today?

_____

_____

Tomorrow I choose:

_____

Day #229

1. What qualities do people look up to you for?

_____

_____

2. Who is someone you look up to and why? Explain.

_____

_____

_____

3. Do you believe that it is important to have someone to look up to? Why or why not?

_____

_____

_____

4. What are the biggest improvements you have made in your life over the past month? Explain.

_____

_____

_____

5. What are the 5 things that you are most grateful for today?

_____

_____

Tomorrow I choose:

_____

Day #230

1. When do you feel most loved?

_____

_____

2. How do you express love to others? Explain.

_____

_____

_____

3. What is one personal quality that you are working on improving and why?

_____

_____

_____

4. If you were given $1,000 but you had to spend it on someone other than you, who would you spend it on and what would you buy them?

_____

_____

_____

5. What are the 5 things that you are most grateful for today?

_____

_____

Tomorrow I choose:

_____

Day #231

1. Think of one of your best friends. What are 5 of their best character traits?

1. _____ 4. _____

2. _____ 5. _____

3. _____

2. What is one quality or trait of yours that has increased by being around this friend?

_____

_____

3. Is there anyone in your life who depletes your energy when you are around them? Explain. ♡

_____

_____

_____

4. Who is the most positive person in your life? Explain what makes them so positive.

_____

_____

5. What are the 5 things that you are most grateful for today?

_____

_____

Tomorrow I choose:

_____

_____

♡ Tip: It is important to spend as much time as possible with people who cause your energy to increase. It is also important to be mindful of your own energy and how it affects others. Become the energy you wish to be surrounded by.

Day #232

1. Did you exhibit confidence today? Explain how you did or how you struggled.

_____

_____

2. What does it feel like to be confident? Explain.

_____

_____

_____

3. What is an area of your life where you are struggling to be confident? Explain.

_____

_____

_____

4. What can you remind yourself of right now that will help you to be more confident?

_____

_____

_____

5. What are the 5 things that you are most grateful for today?

_____

_____

Tomorrow I choose:

_____

Day #233

1. How are you unique?

_____

_____

_____

2. What do you like most and least about your uniqueness? Explain.

_____

_____

_____

3. On a scale of 1 to 10 (10 being the highest) how would you rate your level of self-acceptance?

_____

4. In what areas of your life would you like to be more self-accepting? Explain.

_____

_____

_____

5. What are the 5 things that you are most grateful for today?

_____

_____

_____

Tomorrow I choose:

_____

Day #234

1. What are you looking most forward to short-term in your life and why?

_____

_____

2. What are you looking most forward to long-term in your life and why?

_____

_____

3. Do you feel anxious about anything in the near or far future? Explain.

_____

_____

_____

4. How can you choose to be more confident about the future? ♡

_____

_____

♡ Tip: Remember that you get to choose how you look at your life. The quality of your thoughts directly impacts the quality of your emotions. If you want to rid yourself of anxiety and worry, the key is to stay in the present moment, not overthinking the future. Goals are great to set but do not dwell on the finality of the outcome but rather be committed to doing your best moment by moment. The future has not happened but what you do in the "now" will make a difference tomorrow.

5. What are the 5 things that you are most grateful for today?

_____

_____

_____

Tomorrow I choose:

_____

_____

Day #235

1. Who is the warmest person that you know? Explain how they exude warmth.

_____

_____

_____

2. Would you consider yourself a warm person? Why or why not?

_____

_____

_____

3. If you could help one person to be more warm and loving, who would it be and why?

_____

_____

4. When did you feel appreciated today? Explain.

_____

_____

_____

5. What are the 5 things that you are most grateful for today?

_____

_____

Tomorrow I choose:

_____

Day #236

1. What makes you feel proud of yourself?

_____

_____

_____

2. What is something that you have struggled with that you are choosing to accept and release today?

_____

_____

_____

3. What does it feel like to release something that you have been holding onto?

_____

_____

4. What are 3 things that inspire you to be the best version of yourself and why?

1. _____

2. _____

3. _____

5. What are the 5 things that you are most grateful for today?

_____

_____

Tomorrow I choose:

_____

Day #237

1. What was the highlight of your day today? Explain.

_____

_____

2. Did you struggle with anything today? Explain.

_____

_____

3. Over the past couple of months, have you experienced an improvement in your relationships? Explain why or why not.

_____

_____

_____

4. Where would you like to see improvements in your relationships moving forward? Explain.

_____

_____

_____

5. What are the 5 things that you are most grateful for today?

_____

_____

Tomorrow I choose:

_____

Day #238

1. Who are the 5 closest people to you and how would you rate their energy? Use a P for Positive and N for Negative. ♡

1. _____   4. _____

2. _____   5. _____

3. _____

2. Who is someone that you realize you need to spend less time with and why?

_____

_____

_____

3. Who is someone that you realize you would benefit from spending more time with and why?

_____

_____

4. Do you consider your energy as more positive or negative in general, and how do you feel about it? Explain.

_____

_____

5. What are the 5 things that you are most grateful for today?

_____

_____

♡ Tip: You become the company you keep. Spend more time with positive people and you will feel happier and more inspired.

Tomorrow I choose:

_____

Day #239

1. What were your happiest moments today?

_____

_____

2. How does it feel to focus on what went well during the day? Explain.

_____

_____

3. What are 3 positive thoughts that get your mindset back on track when you are not feeling happy? Explain. ♡

_____

_____

4. If you could have 3 thoughts that do not serve you erased from your mind, what would they be and how would erasing them benefit your life? ♥

_____

_____

_____

5. What are the 5 things that you are most grateful for today?

_____

_____

Tomorrow I choose:

_____

♡ Tip: Anytime that you observe a positive thought that makes you feel good, think of a "save" button on your mental computer keyboard and click it. This will create a memory folder of positive thoughts that you can open when you need them.

♥ Tip: Once you recognize thought patterns that do not serve you, you have the power to shift them when they arise. Anytime these thoughts come up, envision that you have a delete button that you can click to remove the thought and a save button for positive ones. Remember you cannot control what happens around you, but you can control how you respond to it.

Day #240

1. Looking back, what do you recall as being your best day ever? Explain in detail what happened.

_____

_____

_____

2. Using at least 5 adjectives, describe what feeling good feels like to you?

_____

_____

_____

3. What qualities make you a leader?

_____

_____

4. Who is the most effective leader you know, and what makes them a good leader?

_____

_____

_____

5. What are the 5 things that you are most grateful for today?

_____

_____

Tomorrow I choose:

_____

Day #241

1. How were you helpful today? Explain.

_____

_____

2. How did being helpful feel?

_____

_____

_____

3. What makes you unstoppable? Give details.

_____

_____

_____

4. How do you feel when you look at your super strengths? Explain.

_____

_____

_____

5. What are the 5 things that you are most grateful for today?

_____

_____

Tomorrow I choose:

_____

Day #242

1. What are the qualities that you appreciate most in your parents or caretakers? ♡

_____

_____

_____

2. What is one way that your parents or caretakers could improve how they are raising you? Explain.

_____

_____

_____

3. Would you be willing to share this feeling with them? Why or why not.

_____

_____

4. What are 3 freedoms that you are blessed to have?

1. _____

2. _____

3. _____

5. What are the 5 things that you are most grateful for today?

_____

_____

♡ Tip: Sharing your appreciation with your loved ones will naturally fuel your heart with greater happiness.

Tomorrow I choose:

_____

Day #243

1. What life experience have you gone through that changed your life in an incredibly powerful way? Explain in detail.

_____

_____

_____

2. How did you personally change from that experience?

_____

_____

3. What is something that you have been told by an adult that you realize that you don't agree with? Explain.

_____

_____

_____

4. Who do you look up to most and why?

_____

_____

5. What are the 5 things that you are most grateful for today?

_____

_____

Tomorrow I choose:

_____

Day #244

1. Over the next few days, what 5 things are you most looking forward to?

1. _____

2. _____

3. _____

4. _____

5. _____

2. What are your 5 greatest strengths?

1. _____ 4. _____

2. _____ 5. _____

3. _____

3. Over the last couple of weeks, how have you improved in how you deal with anger or frustration? Explain.

_____

4. What is one piece of advice that you received recently that improved your life? Explain how your life improved.

_____

_____

5. What are the 5 things that you are most grateful for today?

_____

Tomorrow I choose:

_____

Day #245

1. Over the past few days, when have you felt frustrated? Explain an instance.

_____

_____

2. What is one way that you previously handled frustration, which you have replaced with something more effective? Give details.

_____

_____

_____

3. How do you feel when you experience the benefits of your personal growth? Explain.

_____

_____

4. What talent have you recently found that you have? If you haven't found one, share a talent that you would like to have. Explain.

_____

_____

_____

5. What are the 5 things that you are most grateful for today?

_____

_____

Tomorrow I choose:

_____

Day #246

1. Who are the 5 most positive people in your life and what traits make each of them this way?

_____

_____

_____

_____

2. How do you show appreciation to your most cherished family and friends?

_____

_____

3. What have you done in the past 24 hours to be kind, and how did it feel?

_____

_____

_____

4. When did you feel your best today? What were you doing? Explain. ♡

_____

_____

5. What are the 5 things that you are most grateful for today?

_____

_____

♡ Tip: Remember when you feel your best, so the next time that you are not feeling as great you can choose something that feels better.

Tomorrow I choose:

_____

Day #247

1. When do you feel your most confident? Explain.

_____

_____

_____

2. What are 5 adjectives that describe how your heart feels when it is happy?

_____

_____

_____

3. What are 5 adjectives that describe how your heart feels when it is unhappy?

_____

_____

_____

4. What has been the most transformative experience for you while doing this journal so far? Explain.

_____

_____

5. What are the 5 things that you are most grateful for today?

_____

_____

Tomorrow I choose:

_____

Day #248

1. If you could be anywhere right now, where would you want to be and what would you be doing?

_____

_____

_____

2. What is a feeling that you would like to experience every day? Explain.

_____

_____

_____

3. What is preventing you from experiencing that feeling daily? Explain.

_____

_____

_____

4. How can you improve your likelihood of feeling the desired feeling more often?

_____

_____

5. What are the 5 things that you are most grateful for today?

_____

_____

_____

Tomorrow I choose:

_____

Day #249

1. What is the hardest thing that you have ever had to do? Explain.

_____

_____

_____

2. How did that experience impact your life emotionally?

_____

_____

_____

3. What is something that you want to do but you are too afraid to try? Give details.

_____

_____

4. Write yourself a pep talk to encourage yourself to try despite your fears.

_____

_____

_____

5. What are the 5 things that you are most grateful for today?

_____

_____

Tomorrow I choose:

_____

Day #250

1. What is going well in your life right now? Explain.

_____

_____

2. What is the most negative thought in your mind right now?

_____

_____

3. Do you tend to pay more attention to what is going well in your life or to the negative thoughts? Explain. ♡

_____

_____

_____

4. When you mentally click on "save" for your positive thoughts and "delete" for the negative ones, what happens? Explain.

_____

_____

_____

5. What are the 5 things that you are most grateful for today?

_____

_____

♡ Tip: Remember to mentally "save" the positive thoughts and click "delete" on the negative ones. Focus on what feels good and you will feel even better.

Tomorrow I choose:

_____

Day #251

1. Write a thank you letter to yourself, focusing on your mind, body, and feelings. Express your appreciation.

_____

_____

_____

2. How does it feel to express gratitude to yourself?

_____

_____

3. Would you describe yourself as courageous? Explain why or why not.

_____

_____

4. What is the most courageous thing that you have ever done? Explain in detail what happened and how you felt.

_____

_____

_____

5. What are the 5 things that you are most grateful for today?

_____

_____

Tomorrow I choose:

_____

Day #252

1. Share 5 moments from over the past year when you can say that you were truly happy:

1. _____

2. _____

3. _____

4. _____

5. _____

2. What have you identified as personal triggers of anxiety and overthinking in your life?

_____

_____

3. What positive ways have you learned to cope with anxiety and overthinking?

_____

_____

4. How has your life improved due to these better coping mechanisms?

_____

_____

5. What are the 5 things that you are most grateful for today?

_____

_____

Tomorrow I choose:

_____

Day #253

1. Think of someone who has caused you pain. What happened? Explain.

_____

_____

2. Write this person a letter of forgiveness (you can share it or keep it private). ♡

_____

_____

_____

3. Do you find it easy to forgive those who have wronged you? Explain why or why not.

_____

_____

_____

4. Who would you like to receive forgiveness from and why? Explain what happened.

_____

_____

_____

5. What are the 5 things that you are most grateful for today?

_____

_____

Tomorrow I choose:

_____

♡ Tip: Forgiveness of yourself and others is important to freeing your heart and mind from resentment and guilt. It is the only true pathway to inner peace and healing.

Day #254

1. What do you look forward to the most when thinking about your future? Give details.

_____

_____

_____

2. What animal do you feel you are most similar to and why? Explain.

_____

_____

_____

3. Have you ever missed an opportunity? Explain what happened.

_____

_____

_____

4. What would you do to not miss an opportunity in the future?

_____

_____

5. What are the 5 things that you are most grateful for today?

_____

_____

Tomorrow I choose:

_____

Day #255

1. What is something that you do regularly to keep yourself healthy?

_____

_____

2. On a scale of 1 to 10 (10 being the best) how is your self-esteem today, and how do you feel overall? Explain.

_____

_____

3. When you look at yourself in the mirror, how do you feel? Share your observations.

_____

_____

_____

4. What are 3 affirmations that you need to hear right now? Write them down and then speak them to yourself while looking in a mirror.

1. _____

2. _____

3. _____

5. What are the 5 things that you are most grateful for today?

_____

_____

Tomorrow I choose:

_____

Day #256

1. If you ruled the world, what would be the first 3 things that you would do as ruler?

_____

_____

_____

_____

2. When have you felt sad over the past few days? Explain what happened.

_____

_____

3. When did you feel your happiest over the past few days? Explain what happened.

_____

_____

4. What are a few ways that you help yourself to feel better when you are feeling down?

_____

_____

_____

5. What are the 5 things that you are most grateful for today?

_____

_____

Tomorrow I choose:

_____

Day #257

1. Do you enjoy learning? Explain why or why not.

_____

_____

_____

2. What could your teachers do to make your learning more effective for you?

_____

_____

_____

3. What is one good deed that you are committed to doing this week? Explain.

_____

_____

4. When is the last time someone did something nice for you? What happened and how did you feel?

_____

_____

_____

5. What are the 5 things that you are most grateful for today?

_____

_____

Tomorrow I choose:

_____

Day #258

1. If you could live anywhere in the world, where would you live and why would you want to live there?

_____

_____

_____

2. What do you appreciate most about your life and why?

_____

_____

3. What are you currently struggling with? Explain.

_____

_____

_____

4. What is a way that you can get support to help you with your struggle? Explain.

_____

_____

_____

5. What are the 5 things that you are most grateful for today?

_____

_____

Tomorrow I choose:

_____

Day #259

1. If you could create a holiday, describe what it would it be like and what it would celebrate.

_____

_____

2. If you could trade one aspect of your personality for something else, what would you get rid of and what would you want in its place?

_____

_____

_____

3. What are a few ideas that you can think of that will help you to let go of the part of your personality that does not serve you? Explain.

_____

_____

_____

4. What was the most inspiring thing that happened today? Give details.

_____

_____

5. What are the 5 things that you are most grateful for today?

_____

_____

Tomorrow I choose:

_____

Day #260

1. What does guilt feel like to you? Explain.

_____

_____

2. Is there anything that you are currently feeling guilty about? If so, explain. If not, explain a time when you experienced feeling guilty.

_____

_____

_____

3. Do you tend to think mostly of the past, the present, or the future? Explain. ♡

_____

_____

4. What are a few ways that you can feel more connected to the present moment? Give at least 4 examples.

_____

_____

_____

♡ Tip: To live in the present is the key to experiencing peace. The past should be for reference and the future for your hopes and dreams. However, if you are more often mentally dwelling in the past, you will be more anxious, and if you're often in the future, you will feel more worried. Let each moment lead you to the next.

5. What are the 5 things that you are most grateful for today?

_____

_____

Tomorrow I choose:

_____

Day #261

1. What are the 5 most selfless things that you have ever done?

_____

_____

_____

2. How does it feel to act selflessly?

_____

_____

3. What is the most selfless act someone has done for you? Explain.

_____

_____

_____

4. How did it feel to experience someone acting selflessly toward you?

_____

_____

_____

5. What are the 5 things that you are most grateful for today?

_____

_____

Tomorrow I choose:

_____

Day #262

1. Do you ever find it difficult to be grateful? Explain.

_____

_____

2. Out of all your more difficult emotions, which one is the most challenging for you to deal with? Explain.

_____

_____

_____

3. When do you feel most empowered? Explain.

_____

_____

4. What are a few ways you have learned to stay balanced and in your power? Give at least 4 examples.

_____

_____

_____

5. What are the 5 things that you are most grateful for today?

_____

_____

Tomorrow I choose:

_____

Day #263

1. What is one way that you took care of yourself today. Explain in detail.

_____

_____

_____

2. How do you feel when you are taking care of yourself? Use at least 3 adjectives to explain.

_____

_____

_____

3. When did you feel most cared for by another recently? What happened?

_____

_____

_____

4. How do you feel when others prioritize your well-being? Explain.

_____

_____

5. What are the 5 things that you are most grateful for today?

_____

_____

Tomorrow I choose:

_____

Day #264

1. What does it mean to have confidence? Explain.

_____

_____

2. How does being confident impact your personal happiness? Explain.

_____

_____

_____

3. What are some areas in your life where you want to grow that you believe will improve your self-confidence? Explain.

_____

_____

_____

4. Where have you gained confidence over the past year that makes you feel happy? Explain.

_____

_____

5. What are the 5 things that you are most grateful for today?

_____

_____

Tomorrow I choose:

_____

Day #265

1. When was the last time that you can remember being dishonest? What happened and why did you choose dishonesty? Explain.

_____

_____

_____

2. Do you struggle with being honest? Why or why not.

_____

_____

3. Do you believe it is important to be honest? Explain.

_____

_____

_____

4. When is a time that you were lied to? What happened and how did you feel?

_____

_____

_____

5. What are the 5 things that you are most grateful for today?

_____

_____

Tomorrow I choose:

_____

Day #266

1. Do you believe that others care about your feelings? Why or why not?

_____

_____

_____

2. Do you care about other people's feelings? Explain.

_____

_____

3. When is a time that you have felt let down by someone, and how did you feel in that moment?

_____

_____

_____

4. Do you believe it is important to follow through on promises? Why or why not.

_____

_____

_____

5. What are the 5 things that you are most grateful for today?

_____

_____

Tomorrow I choose:

_____

Day #267

1. Would you characterize yourself as a person of integrity? Explain why or why not.

_____

_____

2. What does it mean to you to have integrity?

_____

_____

_____

3. Who in your life exemplifies integrity and why?

_____

_____

_____

4. How does it feel to have someone in your life whom you can count on?

_____

_____

_____

5. What are the 5 things that you are most grateful for today?

_____

_____

Tomorrow I choose:

_____

Day #268

1. If you could design tomorrow in any way that you wish, what would your day look like?

_____

_____

_____

2. What made you smile today? Explain.

_____

_____

3. Where in your life do you see the most growth?

_____

_____

_____

4. How does it feel to observe yourself growing and improving?

_____

_____

_____

5. What are the 5 things that you are most grateful for today?

_____

_____

Tomorrow I choose:

_____

Day #269

1. Have you ever experienced betrayal? Explain what happened.

_____

_____

_____

2. Are you able to forgive others when they have hurt you even without an apology? Explain why or why not.

_____

_____

_____

3. How does it feel when you are able to forgive someone?

_____

_____

_____

4. How does it feel when you are forgiven for something?

_____

_____

5. What are the 5 things that you are most grateful for today?

_____

_____

Tomorrow I choose:

_____

Day #270

1. If you could know one thing about the future, what would you want to know and why?

_____

_____

_____

2. What makes you nervous?

_____

_____

3. How do you handle your feelings of nervousness?

_____

_____

4. What is something that you have been working on that has made you feel more peaceful? Explain.

_____

_____

_____

5. What are the 5 things that you are most grateful for today?

_____

_____

Tomorrow I choose:

_____

Day #271

1. What is something that went right for you today? Explain.

_____

_____

2. Is it easy for you to look at the positive things in your life or easier to focus on the negative? Explain.

_____

_____

_____

3. What are a few ways you can choose to find the positives throughout your day?

_____

_____

4. What is the difference in your mood when you look at the positives as opposed to when you look at the negatives? Explain.

_____

_____

_____

5. What are the 5 things that you are most grateful for today?

_____

_____

Tomorrow I choose:

_____

Day #272

1. What are 3 ways that you can exercise self-control when you are feeling triggered?

1. _____

2. _____

3. _____

2. What are your 5 greatest character strengths?

1. _____   4. _____

2. _____   5. _____

3. _____

3. Do you believe that acknowledging your strengths helps you to feel better about yourself? Explain why or why not.

_____

_____

4. What is a positive trait you see in someone who you respect that you would like to personally improve on and why?

_____

_____

5. What are the 5 things that you are most grateful for today?

_____

_____

Tomorrow I choose:

_____

Day #273

1. How do you think others view you? Explain.

_____

_____

2. Do you believe others generally understand you accurately? Explain why or why not.

_____

_____

_____

3. Are you able to examine yourself when receiving constructive criticism? Explain why or why not.

_____

_____

4. Are you able to express your thoughts and feelings to others when you want to be heard? Explain.

_____

_____

_____

5. What are the 5 things that you are most grateful for today?

_____

_____

Tomorrow I choose:

_____

Day #274

1. When was a time that you recently felt sad? Share the experience.

_____

_____

2. What helps you get through times of sadness?

_____

_____

3. Do you feel that you are able to accept your feelings of sadness or do you try to push them away? Explain.

_____

_____

_____

4. What is one way that you handle sadness in a self-loving way, and what is one way you handle sadness in a self-defeating way?

_____

_____

_____

5. What are the 5 things that you are most grateful for today?

_____

_____

Tomorrow I choose:

_____

Day #275

1. List 5 things that make you smile:

1. _____

2. _____

3. _____

4. _____

5. _____

2. What is something that you can remember when life feels tough?

_____

_____

3. What is something that you need to hear today? ♡

_____

_____

4. How does it feel to express what you need to hear?

_____

5. What are the 5 things that you are most grateful for today?

_____

_____

Tomorrow I choose:

_____

♡ Tip: Asking yourself these questions leads you to self-care and realizing that you are powerful and capable of supporting yourself. This does not mean you shouldn't seek support from others, but it does mean that in moments where you want to understand your needs, you are able to recognize them. Treat yourself as you would your best friend.

Day #276

1. What are 5 songs that instantly lift your mood? ♡

1. _____

2. _____

3. _____

4. _____

5. _____

2. What makes your heart feel peaceful? Explain.

_____

_____

3. What is something that you appreciate about yourself that no one knows?

_____

_____

4. What is one moment today where you were fully present? Explain.

_____

_____

♡ Tip: Whenever you are down and struggling, play these songs and picture your heart feeling peaceful, optimistic, and happy. The best way to do this is through an attitude of gratitude, while choosing to do things that bring out the best in you as opposed to the stress in you.

5. What are the 5 things that you are most grateful for today?

_____

_____

Tomorrow I choose:

_____

Day #277

1. What was your favorite moment today? What happened and what emotions did you experience in this moment?

_____

_____

_____

2. What has been your greatest personal accomplishment over the past few weeks?

_____

_____

3. Are you kind to yourself? Explain why or why not.

_____

_____

4. What would happen if there was no social media? Would this be a good thing or a bad thing?

_____

_____

_____

5. What are the 5 things that you are most grateful for today?

_____

_____

Tomorrow I choose:

_____

Day #278

1. What is something that you believe would improve your life if you spent more time focused on it and why?

_____

_____

_____

2. What is something that you believe would improve your life if you spent less time focused on it and why?

_____

_____

_____

3. When do you feel most optimistic? Explain.

_____

_____

4. When do you feel most pessimistic? Explain.

_____

_____

5. What are the 5 things that you are most grateful for today?

_____

_____

Tomorrow I choose:

_____

Day #279

1. What is something that you are currently struggling with? Explain.

_____

_____

2. How do you think your life would be without this struggle?

_____

_____

3. What can you appreciate about the struggle that you are facing? What has it taught you? Explain.

_____

_____

4. Imagine that you had the biggest supporter who loved you more than anything and saw you for all that you are. What would they say to you to encourage you during this challenging time? Be descriptive!

_____

_____

_____

5. What are the 5 things that you are most grateful for today?

_____

_____

Tomorrow I choose:

_____

Day #280

1. Over the past few days, when have you felt overwhelmed? Explain what was going on.

_____

_____

2. How did you handle feeling overwhelmed?

_____

_____

3. In your opinion, did you handle your feelings in a healthy way? Explain why or why not.

_____

_____

_____

4. What is something that you learned about yourself in this situation that will help you in the future?

_____

_____

_____

5. What are the 5 things that you are most grateful for today?

_____

_____

Tomorrow I choose:

_____

Day #281

1. Do you feel a sense of belonging in your life? Explain.

_____

_____

2. Describe a time in your life where you really felt like you belonged and were accepted.

_____

_____

_____

3. Describe a time in your life where you didn't feel as though you belonged or were not accepted.

_____

_____

_____

4. Do you need the approval of your peers to feel accepted? Explain why or why not.

_____

_____

_____

5. What are the 5 things that you are most grateful for today?

_____

_____

Tomorrow I choose:

_____

Day #282

1. When is the last time that you recall feeling jealous? Explain what happened.

_____

_____

2. Describe, using at least 4 adjectives, how jealousy feels to you.

_____

_____

_____

3. Do you find yourself comparing your life to the life of others? Explain why or why not.

_____

_____

_____

4. How has owning and identifying your feelings helped you compare yourself with others less? Explain.

_____

_____

_____

5. What are the 5 things that you are most grateful for today?

_____

_____

Tomorrow I choose:

_____

Day #283

1. When you think of happiness, what immediately comes to mind? Explain.

_____

_____

_____

2. Do you believe that you can choose to be happy? Explain why or why not.

_____

_____

3. When was the last time where you felt happy all day? Explain your day in detail.

_____

_____

_____

4. What tools have helped you improve your experience of happiness?

_____

_____

_____

5. What are the 5 things that you are most grateful for today?

_____

_____

Tomorrow I choose:

_____

Day #284

1. When you make a mistake, how do you feel?

_____

_____

2. Do you strive to be "perfect" or do you believe that doing your best is enough? Explain. ♡

_____

_____

_____

3. Do you feel worthy of goodness? Explain why or why not.

_____

_____

4. What are 5 of your character traits that you are most proud of?

1._____   4._____

2._____   5._____

3._____

5. What are the 5 things that you are most grateful for today?

♡ Tip: There is no perfect person in the world. Part of the gift of life is getting to learn through your mistakes and growing to love yourself despite your flaws. When you can accept yourself, you are able to know your worth. When you know your worth, you are in your power.

_____

_____

Tomorrow I choose:

_____

Day #285

1. What is a past hurt that you are having trouble letting go of? Explain.

_____

_____

2. Close your eyes and think of something that someone could say or do that would help you release this past hurt. Share what came up for you.

_____

_____

3. Take a deep breath and visualize where you feel this hurt in your body. Now close your eyes and say, "I accept that I feel hurt" and move the hurt from where it is into your heart. Keep repeating the words of acceptance until you have moved the hurt into your heart. Now share what you experienced. How did you feel? Was it challenging or pretty easy? Give details.

_____

_____

_____

4. How are you feeling now? Do you still feel the hurt? Explain in detail. ♡

_____

_____

5. What are the 5 things that you are most grateful for today?

_____

_____

Tomorrow I choose:

_____

♡ Tip: This happy heart practice is something that you can use at all times. Whenever you have a feeling that you are struggling with, you can use this tool to connect with your heart and heal.

Day #286

1. What surprised you in a good way today? Explain.

_____

_____

2. What does it feel like when something unexpectedly awesome happens?

_____

_____

_____

3. What does it feel like when something unexpectedly negative happens, and how do you generally react?

_____

_____

_____

4. Do you fear the unknown? Why or why not?

_____

_____

_____

5. What are the 5 things that you are most grateful for today?

_____

_____

Tomorrow I choose:

_____

Day #287

1. If you could be any famous person for the day, who would you be and what would you do?

_____

_____

_____

2. If there was nothing you couldn't do, what would you do? Explain.

_____

_____

_____

3. Do you consider yourself more fearless or fearful? Explain.

_____

_____

4. What can you do today that will help you believe in yourself with greater confidence?

_____

_____

_____

5. What are the 5 things that you are most grateful for today?

_____

_____

Tomorrow I choose:

_____

Day #288

1. Are you able to take ownership for your mistakes or do you find yourself blaming others? Explain.

_____

_____

_____

2. Have you ever been blamed for something you did not do? If so, explain what happened and how you felt.

_____

_____

_____

3. Does a fear of failure hold you back in any area(s) in your life? Why or why not.

_____

_____

4. What can you commit to today that will help you to be less fearful? Explain.

_____

_____

5. What are the 5 things that you are most grateful for today?

_____

_____

Tomorrow I choose:

_____

Day #289

1. What are your 5 most prioritized values?

1. _____   4. _____

2. _____   5. _____

3. _____

2. Do you believe that you generally stay true to your values? Explain why or why not.

_____

_____

_____

3. What value have you been most likely to compromise? Explain.

_____

_____

_____

4. How can you live with a greater commitment to your prioritized values? Explain.

_____

_____

_____

5. What are the 5 things that you are most grateful for today?

_____

_____

Tomorrow I choose:

_____

Day #290

1. Did you do your best today? Explain.

_____

_____

2. How do you feel when you give your best?

_____

_____

_____

3. What does positive energy feel like?

_____

_____

_____

4. What does negative energy feel like?

_____

_____

_____

5. What are the 5 things that you are most grateful for today?

_____

_____

Tomorrow I choose:

_____

Day #291

1. What inspired you today? Explain what happened.

_____

_____

2. How were you an inspiration over the past few days?

_____

_____

_____

3. What does it feel like when you receive affirmations from others?

_____

_____

_____

4. What is the last affirmation you received, and who was it from?

_____

_____

_____

5. What are the 5 things that you are most grateful for today?

_____

_____

Tomorrow I choose:

_____

Day #292

1. What is something that you are currently struggling with? Explain.

_____

_____

_____

2. What have you been doing to deal with this struggle in a positive way?

_____

_____

3. If you could snap your fingers and make something happen in this moment to help your heart, what would you make happen? Explain.

_____

_____

_____

4. What did you observe today that made you smile?

_____

_____

_____

5. What are the 5 things that you are most grateful for today?

_____

_____

Tomorrow I choose:

_____

Day #293

1. Do you find yourself reacting to things that upset you? Explain.

_____

_____

2. What is one way that you could handle how you deal with upsetting situations better?

_____

_____

_____

3. What is at least one way that you handle difficult situations? Give as many examples as you can think of.

_____

_____

_____

4. What is an obstacle you have overcome in your life that you are proud of? Explain.

_____

_____

_____

5. What are the 5 things that you are most grateful for today?

_____

_____

Tomorrow I choose:

_____

Day #294

1. When is the last time someone talked badly about you behind your back? What happened?

_____

_____

_____

2. How did you feel hearing what was said about you?

_____

_____

_____

3. What do you think about gossip? Explain.

_____

_____

_____

4. Do you find yourself getting involved in gossip with others? Explain.

_____

_____

5. What are the 5 things that you are most grateful for today?

_____

_____

Tomorrow I choose:

_____

Day #295

1. How did you exhibit an attitude of gratitude today? What happened?

_____

_____

2. How does it feel when you live in gratitude as opposed to thanklessness? Explain.

_____

_____

_____

3. Where in your life could you be more grateful? Explain.

_____

_____

_____

4. How do you express gratitude to others? Give details.

_____

_____

_____

5. What are the 5 things that you are most grateful for today?

_____

_____

Tomorrow I choose:

_____

Day #296

1. If you could do anything fun right now, what would you do and who would you do it with?

_____

_____

2. Do you believe that life should feel good? Why or why not?

_____

_____

3. What are your 5 best attributes?

1. I am: _____   4. I am: _____

2. I am: _____   5. I am: _____

3. I am: _____

4. Close your eyes and envision yourself in a peaceful and beautiful garden for about 5 minutes while breathing steadily. Once you open your eyes, write down what you experienced and how it felt.

_____

_____

_____

5. What are the 5 things that you are most grateful for today?

_____

_____

Tomorrow I choose:

_____

Day #297

1. When did you feel most loved over the past week? Explain what happened.

_____

_____

2. If nothing was holding you back, how would you express your love to others? Explain.

_____

_____

3. Who out of your family or friends knows how to speak love to you the best, and how do they express it?

_____

_____

_____

4. If you could receive more love from any one person, who would it be and how would this impact your life?

_____

_____

_____

5. What are the 5 things that you are most grateful for today?

_____

_____

Tomorrow I choose:

_____

Day #298

1. When do you feel yourself getting defensive? Explain.

_____

_____

2. What emotions do you feel when you react defensively?

_____

_____

3. What are a couple of areas in your life where you could become less defensive?

_____

_____

_____

4. Write at least 3 sentences that describe who you are as a person.

_____

_____

_____

_____

5. What are the 5 things that you are most grateful for today?

_____

_____

Tomorrow I choose:

_____

Day #299

1. What are a few ways that you have changed for the better over the past year? Explain.

_____

_____

2. How does it feel to see these improvements in your life?

_____

_____

_____

3. What is something that you are still working on improving?

_____

_____

_____

4. How do you think that improvement will impact your life? Explain.

_____

_____

_____

5. What are the 5 things that you are most grateful for today?

_____

_____

Tomorrow I choose:

_____

Day #300

1. What does rejection feel like? Explain.

_____

_____

_____

2. When is the last time you felt rejected? What happened?

_____

_____

3. What does being included by others feel like to you? Explain.

_____

_____

_____

4. Share a time that you really felt included by others and how that experience affected you.

_____

_____

_____

5. What are the 5 things that you are most grateful for today?

_____

_____

Tomorrow I choose:

_____

Day #301

1. When did you feel at your very best over the past week? Explain.

_____

_____

2. What do you recognize about your mindset when you are at your best? Explain.

_____

_____

_____

3. Are you able to accept yourself when you aren't at your best? Explain why or why not. ♡

_____

_____

_____

4. What do you struggle with accepting about yourself? Explain.

_____

_____

5. What are the 5 things that you are most grateful for today?

_____

_____

Tomorrow I choose:

_____

♡ Tip: It is impossible to be at your best every single day, but it is possible to accept every single day as an opportunity to be inspired to grow. You actually grow more from the challenging days than from the great days. Remember to see the value of those more difficult days as an opportunity for reflection and growth.

Day #302

1. Do you look at your life as more full or empty? Explain why.

_____

_____

2. What does feeling fulfilled mean to you?

_____

_____

_____

3. Where does a feeling of emptiness show up in your life, and what does that feel like?

_____

_____

_____

4. What are a few ways that you can fill your cup (life) with more goodness and positivity? ♡

_____

♡ Tip: You cannot pour from an empty cup, so it is important that you take the time you need to take care of yourself. Caring about yourself emotionally, mentally, and physically is how you can add more fulfillment to your life. An attitude of gratitude heightens your sense of wellness too. When you invest in your well-being, you will find life to work in your favor with greater ease.

5. What are the 5 things that you are most grateful for today?

_____

_____

Tomorrow I choose:

_____

Day #303

1. What is one thing that you did today that represented your character strengths? Explain in detail.

_____

_____

_____

2. How do you feel when you are acting in a way that is aligned with your strengths? Explain.

_____

_____

_____

3. What color best describes your mood today and why?

_____

_____

4. What color do you want your mood to reflect tomorrow and why?

_____

_____

5. What are the 5 things that you are most grateful for today?

_____

_____

Tomorrow I choose:

_____

Day #304

1. What distractions are hindering your life? Explain.

_____

_____

2. What can you do today to make your life feel more focused with less distractions?

_____

_____

_____

3. When your mind is in focus, what do you see clearly for your life? Give details.

_____

_____

_____

4. When your life is out of focus, what feelings do you experience?

_____

_____

_____

5. What are the 5 things that you are most grateful for today?

_____

_____

Tomorrow I choose:

_____

Day #305

1. Describe in detail what you want your life to look like in 5 years. Be as descriptive as possible.

_____

_____

2. If you could change something about your life right now, what would it be and how would changing it improve life as you know it?

_____

_____

3. Do you consider yourself optimistic about your future? Explain why or why not.

_____

_____

_____

4. What is one personal strength that you can use to make an impact in the world? Explain what it is and how you will use it to make a difference in the world.

_____

_____

_____

5. What are the 5 things that you are most grateful for today?

_____

_____

Tomorrow I choose:

_____

Day #306

1. What is something that you have a tendency to overthink? Explain.

_____

_____

2. What feelings do you experience when you overthink, and how do those feelings affect your life?

_____

_____

_____

3. How would your life improve if you drastically reduced how much you overthink?

_____

_____

4. When was a recent time that you were completely present and in the moment; not thinking about the past or future? Explain in detail and include how you felt.

_____

_____

_____

5. What are the 5 things that you are most grateful for today?

_____

_____

Tomorrow I choose:

_____

Day #307

1. What is one thing that has happened recently that made your heart feel happy? Explain.

_____

_____

2. Do you believe that you let what's happening outside of you determine how you feel on the inside? Explain why or why not.

_____

_____

_____

3. When do you feel the most powerful? Explain.

_____

_____

4. In your opinion, what does it mean to be living in your power? Explain.

_____

_____

_____

5. What are the 5 things that you are most grateful for today?

_____

_____

Tomorrow I choose:

_____

Day #308

1. What are 5 ways that you have changed for the better over the past 6 months?

1. _____

2. _____

3. _____

4. _____

5. _____

2. What is one limiting belief that is holding you back? Explain.

_____

_____

3. What do you believe would change for you if you didn't have this limiting belief? Explain.

_____

_____

4. What can you do today to help release this limiting belief?

_____

_____

5. What are the 5 things that you are most grateful for today?

_____

_____

Tomorrow I choose:

_____

Day #309

1. What are 5 simple things that brighten your day?

1. _____

2. _____

3. _____

4. _____

5. _____

2. Do you generally look for these simple pleasures or more often look at what isn't pleasing or going right? Explain.

_____

_____

3. What is one thing that stood out to you today that made you appreciate your life? Explain.

_____

_____

4. Do you find it difficult to appreciate your life? Explain why or why not.

_____

_____

5. What are the 5 things that you are most grateful for today?

_____

Tomorrow I choose:

_____

Day #310

1. If you could sit down with your older and wiser self, what would you ask yourself?

_____

_____

_____

2. In thinking about what you would ask yourself, is there anything that you realize that will help you in your life right now? Explain.

_____

_____

_____

3. Who in your life has surprised you the most in a positive way? Explain.

_____

_____

_____

4. In what ways do you think that you surprise people?

_____

_____

5. What are the 5 things that you are most grateful for today?

_____

_____

Tomorrow I choose:

_____

Day #311

1. If you could go on an adventure, what would you do and where would you go? Give details.

_____

_____

_____

_____

2. What are 3 important goals that you have achieved in your life?

1. _____

2. _____

3. _____

3. What is a goal that you are putting a lot of work into accomplishing right now?

_____

_____

4. How do you think you will feel when you accomplish this goal?

_____

_____

5. What are the 5 things that you are most grateful for today?

_____

_____

Tomorrow I choose:

_____

Day #312

1. In thinking about your future, what career do you see yourself doing and what excites you about this profession?

_____

_____

_____

2. How do you envision your adult life? Give detail on both your personal and professional vision.

_____

_____

_____

3. What excites you the most about your future and why?

_____

_____

4. What scares you when you think about your future and why?

_____

_____

5. What are the 5 things that you are most grateful for today?

_____

_____

Tomorrow I choose:

_____

Day #313

1. If you could give 3 people each a gift, who would you choose to gift and what would you give them?

_____

_____

_____

2. What individual qualities about these people inspire you?

_____

_____

_____

3. If you could read one person's mind, who would you choose and why?

_____

_____

_____

4. What was the most fun part of your day? Explain.

_____

_____

5. What are the 5 things that you are most grateful for today?

_____

_____

Tomorrow I choose:

_____

Day #314

1. Do you believe in miracles? Why or why not?

_____

_____

_____

2. Have you ever experienced a miracle? If so, explain what happened. If not, what is a miracle that you hope for? Explain.

_____

_____

3. When things aren't going your way, do you believe things will get better or fear that they will get worse? Explain.

_____

_____

_____

4. In thinking about your character, what do you know to be true?

_____

_____

5. What are the 5 things that you are most grateful for today?

_____

_____

Tomorrow I choose:

_____

Day #315

1. Using your 5 senses, describe positivity:

1. Positivity smells like: _____

2. Positivity tastes like: _____

3. Positivity feels like: _____

4. Positivity looks like: _____

5. Positivity sounds like: _____

2. When you are in a positive mindset, how does your daily life differ from when you are in a negative mindset? Explain.

_____

_____

3. What are a few ways that you can start your day on a positive note?

_____

_____

4. What 3 people in your life have the most positive energy, and how do you feel when you are around them?

_____

_____

5. What are the 5 things that you are most grateful for today?

_____

Tomorrow I choose:

_____

Day #316

1. What did you do today that you were most proud of and why?

_____

_____

2. Is there anything you regret from today? Explain why or why not.

_____

_____

_____

3. What do you envision your life looking like one year from now? Explain in detail.

_____

_____

_____

4. If you could spend the day with someone from history, who would it be, what would you do, and why would you choose this person?

_____

_____

_____

5. What are the 5 things that you are most grateful for today?

_____

_____

Tomorrow I choose:

_____

Day #317

1. If you could help one person, who would it be and how would you help them?

_____

_____

2. What does it feel like when people help you when you are in need? Explain.

_____

_____

_____

3. What does it feel like when you are in need and there doesn't seem to be anyone who can help you?

_____

_____

_____

4. What are 3 ways you could ask for help when you need it?

1. _____

2. _____

3. _____

5. What are the 5 things that you are most grateful for today?

_____

_____

Tomorrow I choose:

_____

Day #318

1. On a scale of 1 to 10 (10 being the most), how often do you think that you complain?

_____

2. When is the last time you recall complaining? Explain the situation.

_____

_____

_____

3. Do you believe that there is any benefit to complaining? Explain why or why not.

_____

_____

_____

4. When you hear others complaining, how do you feel and what are your thoughts? Explain.

_____

_____

_____

_____

5. What are the 5 things that you are most grateful for today?

_____

_____

Tomorrow I choose:

_____

Day #319

1. Do you believe it is important to be respectful to adults? Why or why not?

_____

_____

2. When was the last time that you can remember being disrespectful to an adult? What happened?

_____

_____

3. When you realized that you were being disrespectful, how did you feel?

_____

_____

_____

4. Have you ever felt disrespected? If so, what happened and how did you feel in that situation?

_____

_____

_____

5. What are the 5 things that you are most grateful for today?

_____

_____

Tomorrow I choose:

_____

Day #320

1. What are you most looking forward to tomorrow?

_____

_____

2. When you are feeling sad, what is a source of comfort for you? Explain.

_____

_____

_____

3. What are a couple of ways that you are able to comfort yourself when you are sad?

_____

_____

_____

4. How do you comfort others when they are sad? Give an example.

_____

_____

_____

5. What are the 5 things that you are most grateful for today?

_____

_____

Tomorrow I choose:

_____

Day #321

1. What are a few of your favorite ways to spend your free time?

_____

_____

2. What feelings do you generally feel when you are enjoying your favorite activities? Use at least 3 adjectives to describe.

_____

_____

_____

3. How would you describe yourself to a complete stranger?

_____

_____

_____

4. What quality about yourself helps you the most in life and why? Explain.

_____

_____

_____

5. What are the 5 things that you are most grateful for today?

_____

_____

Tomorrow I choose:

_____

Day #322

1. What are your current 3 top priorities and why?

_____

_____

_____

2. Are you good at prioritizing what is most important to you? Explain why or why not.

_____

_____

3. Reread one of your earlier entries in this journal. What has changed most significantly in your life since then? Explain.

_____

_____

_____

4. How does it feel to look back and reflect upon your personal growth? Explain.

_____

_____

_____

5. What are the 5 things that you are most grateful for today?

_____

_____

Tomorrow I choose:

_____

Day #323

1. What are 5 things that you feel you should spend less time doing?

1. _____

2. _____

3. _____

4. _____

5. _____

2. How would your life improve by following through on doing these things less frequently? Explain.

_____

_____

_____

_____

3. What are 5 things you do regularly that benefit your life?

1. _____

2. _____

3. _____

4. _____

5. _____

(continued on the next page...)

Day #323, continued

4. If you had a box that could save 5 of your most meaningful possessions forever, what items would you put into the box and why?

_____

_____

_____

_____

_____

5. What are the 5 things that you are most grateful for today?

_____

_____

_____

Tomorrow I choose:

_____

_____

Day #324

1. What season most represents your personality and why? Explain using descriptive words.

_____

_____

2. If you could go back and relive one day from the past year over again, what day would it be and why? Explain in detail.

_____

_____

_____

3. What was the best thing that happened today, and how did you feel?

_____

_____

4. Who has been the most supportive friend to you? Explain why.

_____

_____

_____

5. What are the 5 things that you are most grateful for today?

_____

_____

Tomorrow I choose:

_____

Day #325

1. Close your eyes and silence your mind, put your hand over your heart for a couple of minutes. Describe what you felt. Be descriptive, using at least 3 adjectives.

_____

_____

2. If you could reverse something that has happened in history, what would you choose to reverse and why? Explain.

_____

_____

_____

3. If you could write something into the future what would you make happen? Explain why.

_____

_____

4. Do you believe that you can make an impact in the world? Explain why or why not.

_____

_____

_____

5. What are the 5 things that you are most grateful for today?

_____

_____

Tomorrow I choose:

_____

Day #326

1. What is your very favorite smell, and how does smelling it make you feel?

_____

_____

_____

2. What is the kindest thing you did today? Explain.

_____

_____

3. How did you feel when you chose to be kind?

_____

_____

4. What is the kindest thing someone has done for you over the past couple of days? Explain what happened and how it made you feel.

_____

_____

5. What are the 5 things that you are most grateful for today?

_____

_____

Tomorrow I choose:

_____

Day #327

1. What is something that has been causing you stress? Explain.

_____

_____

2. Would you say you have been dealing with the stress in an effective way? Explain why or why not.

_____

_____

_____

3. What adjustments could you make that would likely reduce your stress level? Explain.

_____

_____

4. When did you feel most relaxed today? Explain what you were doing and how you felt.

_____

_____

5. What are the 5 things that you are most grateful for today?

_____

_____

Tomorrow I choose:

_____

Day #328

1. What is an area in your life where you would like to feel relief? Explain.

_____

_____

2. What would you do for the next 24 hours if money was no object?

_____

_____

3. What would you do for the next 24 hours if you had no money, but you could do anything that is free with whomever you want? Explain.

_____

_____

4. What 5 of your qualities are you most proud of and why?

1. _____

2. _____

3. _____

4. _____

5. _____

5. What are the 5 things that you are most grateful for today?

_____

_____

Tomorrow I choose:

_____

Day #329

1. If you could invite 5 people to a dinner party, who would you invite and why?

_____

_____

_____

2. What would you serve at your dinner party? Explain.

_____

_____

_____

3. What would you want to talk about at your dinner party?

_____

_____

_____

4. Did you do your best today? Explain why or why not.

_____

_____

5. What are the 5 things that you are most grateful for today?

_____

_____

Tomorrow I choose:

_____

Day #330

1. What scares you the most?

_____

_____

2. Is there anything you have not told someone that you need to tell them? Explain in detail.

_____

_____

_____

3. What are you afraid might happen if you tell them what you need to say?

_____

_____

_____

4. In looking at your life, what do you think holds you back the most? Explain.

_____

_____

_____

5. What are the 5 things that you are most grateful for today?

_____

_____

Tomorrow I choose:

_____

Day #331

1. What is the best decision that you recently made? Share what happened.

_____

_____

2. Do you think through your decisions before making them or would you say that you are more impulsive? Explain.

_____

_____

_____

3. Describe what makes someone a good decision maker.

_____

_____

_____

4. Do you consider yourself a good decision maker? Why or why not?

_____

_____

_____

5. What are the 5 things that you are most grateful for today?

_____

_____

Tomorrow I choose:

_____

Day #332

1. Using your 5 senses, describe kindness.

1. Kindness feels like: _____

2. Kindness tastes like: _____

3. Kindness sounds like: _____

4. Kindness looks like: _____

5. Kindness smells like: _____

2. Were you kind today? Explain why or why not.

_____

_____

3. What is the kindest thing someone has done for your over the past few days? Share what happened.

_____

_____

4. What act of kindness can you commit to doing tomorrow?

_____

_____

5. What are the 5 things that you are most grateful for today?

_____

_____

Tomorrow I choose:

_____

Day #333

1. If you could ask a question to anyone about anything, what would you ask and to whom would you ask it?

_____

_____

_____

2. Do you feel more different than others or more similar? Explain.

_____

_____

_____

3. On a scale of 1 to 10 (10 being the highest) how would you rate your confidence today? Explain your answer.

_____

_____

4. What is something that you are working on that has increased your confidence? Explain.

_____

_____

5. What are the 5 things that you are most grateful for today?

_____

_____

Tomorrow I choose:

_____

Day #334

1. Do you consider yourself more controlling or more trusting? Explain.

_____

_____

_____

2. In what part of your life do you feel that you are most trusting?

_____

_____

_____

3. Do you struggle with being hard on yourself?

_____

_____

4. How can you choose to be gentler with yourself? Explain.

_____

_____

_____

5. What are the 5 things that you are most grateful for today?

_____

_____

Tomorrow I choose:

_____

Day #335

1. What is something that has recently happened that really upset you? Explain.

_____

_____

_____

2. Do you feel that you have resolved what happened? Explain why or why not.

_____

_____

_____

3. Who is your #1 supporter? Explain why.

_____

_____

4. What qualities do you appreciate most about your #1 supporter?

_____

_____

_____

5. What are the 5 things that you are most grateful for today?

_____

_____

Tomorrow I choose:

_____

Day #336

1. Do you feel ashamed of yourself or your life in any way? Explain what causes you to feel shame or how you resolve shameful feelings so they do not linger.

_____

_____

2. What affirmation can you give yourself right now to help alleviate any burdens that you are carrying? Feel it in your heart and then write your response.

_____

_____

3. What obstacle in your life are you most proud of yourself for overcoming? Explain in detail.

_____

_____

_____

4. When you recognize all that you have overcome, what feelings come up for you? Explain your feelings and any realizations you have.

_____

_____

5. What are the 5 things that you are most grateful for today?

_____

_____

Tomorrow I choose:

_____

Day #337

1. Do you feel a sense of pressure in your life, or do you feel calm? Explain.

_____

_____

2. How would you explain either the calm or pressure you experience, and how is it affecting your everyday life?

_____

_____

_____

3. What are 3 things that bring you a sense of calmness?

1. _____

2. _____

3. _____

4. What was your happiest moment today? Explain in detail what happened.

_____

_____

_____

5. What are the 5 things that you are most grateful for today?

_____

_____

Tomorrow I choose:

_____

Day #338

1. Take a few moments to be silent and observe your thoughts. What thoughts did you observe? Explain.

_____

_____

_____

2. Take a few moments to be silent and feel what is in your heart. How did your heart feel? Explain.

_____

_____

_____

3. Based on your observations of your thoughts, what did you learn?

_____

_____

4. Based on your observations of how your heart feels, what did you learn? ♡

_____

_____

5. What are the 5 things that you are most grateful for today?

_____

_____

Tomorrow I choose:

_____

♡ Tip: Taking the time to observe your thoughts and feelings is a great way to care for yourself and learn about your needs. It is valuable and highly recommended to check in with yourself daily.

Day #339

1. What has been your biggest life change over the past year? Explain in detail.

_____

2. What are 5 ways that your life has improved over the past year? ♡

1. _____

2. _____

3. _____

4. _____

5. _____

3. What are 5 of the most impactful lessons that you have learned over the past year?

1. _____

2. _____

3. _____

4. _____

5. _____

4. What are you most looking forward to over the next 12 months? Give details.

_____

♡ Tip: Life is full of ups and downs and all arounds: however, it is how we choose to look at life that makes all the difference. When you appreciate the good, the good gets better. When you dwell on the bad, the bad gets worse. Choosing to look at the positives will increase your happiness and improve your life.

5. What are the 5 things that you are most grateful for today?

_____

Tomorrow I choose:

_____

Day #340

1. Do you feel that you made good decisions today? Explain why or why not.

_____

_____

2. In what areas in your life do you need to have better boundaries? Explain. ♡

_____

_____

3. Is there anyone in your life who does not respect you? How could you set healthy boundaries to honor yourself and reduce this mistreatment?

_____

_____

_____

4. Is there any area of your life where you feel you have set healthy boundaries? Explain why or why not in detail.

_____

_____

_____

5. What are the 5 things that you are most grateful for today?

_____

_____

Tomorrow I choose:

_____

♡ Tip: Boundaries are knowing and understanding your limits and enforcing them. If you feel overwhelmed or drained by a person or a situation, you likely have not identified appropriate boundaries, if any at all. Anytime you feel uncomfortable in a situation, ask yourself what you have control over and what you can change in the situation. Becoming self-aware and honoring your feelings and needs is critical to reducing stress and drama in your life.

Day #341

1. Is there anyone who you currently feel resentment toward? If so, give details. If not, explain a time where you experienced resentment.

_____

_____

2. How has resentment hindered your life in the past or present? Explain.

_____

_____

_____

3. Do you find it difficult to truly forgive others? Explain why or why not.

_____

_____

_____

4. Picture your life free of any resentment, full of love and compassion. How do you believe life would feel? How would life feel differently than it does right now? Explain in detail.

_____

_____

5. What are the 5 things that you are most grateful for today?

_____

_____

Tomorrow I choose:

_____

Day #342

1. Do you find it difficult to admit when you are wrong? Explain why or why not.

_____

_____

_____

2. On a scale of 1 to 10 (10 being the most), how argumentative would you say you are? Explain your answer.

_____

_____

3. On a scale of 1 to 10 (10 being the most), how understanding would you say you are? Explain your answer.

_____

_____

4. What are 3 examples of how you have adapted to life over the past year?

1. _____

2. _____

3. _____

5. What are the 5 things that you are most grateful for today?

_____

_____

Tomorrow I choose:

_____

Day #343

1. Have you been the kind of friend that you want as a friend? Share your thoughts.

_____

_____

_____

2. Are your closest friends the kind of friends that lift you up or bring you down? Explain.

_____

_____

_____

3. What mistake have you learned the most from? What happened, and what did you learn?

_____

_____

4. Do you have a difficult time being accountable for the mistakes you make? Explain in detail why or why not.

_____

_____

5. What are the 5 things that you are most grateful for today?

_____

_____

Tomorrow I choose:

_____

Day #344

1. Do you get more energized by spending time alone or spending time with others? Explain the energy difference.

_____

_____

_____

_____

2. What are the 10 most helpful things you have learned about yourself while doing this journal?

1. _____

2. _____

3. _____

4. _____

5. _____

6. _____

7. _____

8. _____

9. _____

10. _____

(continued on the next page...)

Day #344, continued

3. What is one area where you have felt an incredible improvement in your life in recent months? Explain.

_____

_____

_____

4. What recent conversation has impacted you the most and why? Explain the situation, including who you were talking to.

_____

_____

_____

_____

5. What are the 5 things that you are most grateful for today?

_____

_____

Tomorrow I choose:

_____

_____

Day #345

1. Do you consider yourself more of a controlling person or more trusting? Explain.

_____

_____

2. In what parts of your life do you feel most trusting?

_____

_____

3. Do you struggle with being hard on yourself? Explain.

_____

_____

4. How could you be gentler with yourself?

_____

_____

5. What are the 5 things that you are most grateful for today?

_____

_____

Tomorrow I choose:

_____

Day #346

1. When do you feel the most connected to your heart?

_____

_____

2. What are some of the things that cause you to go into your head as opposed to your heart? Share some times when your mind has a tendency to take over.

_____

_____

_____

3. Do your feelings ever scare you? Explain why or why not.

_____

_____

4. Do you feel like you have your guard up to keep people from getting close to you? If yes, explain in detail why. If not, explain how you are able to be open and connected.

_____

_____

_____

5. What are the 5 things that you are most grateful for today?

_____

_____

Tomorrow I choose:

_____

Day #347

1. Do you consider yourself an honest person? Explain why or why not.

_____

_____

_____

2. Is it ever ok to be dishonest? Explain your thoughts.

_____

_____

_____

3. When is the last time that you cried? Explain what happened and how you felt.

_____

_____

_____

4. Check in with your heart right now. Explain how you are feeling.

_____

_____

5. What are the 5 things that you are most grateful for today?

_____

_____

Tomorrow I choose:

_____

Day #348

1. When is the last time that you felt frustrated? Explain how you felt and what happened.

_____

_____

2. Are there any emotions that you experience that scare you or that you avoid? Explain in detail.

_____

_____

3. What are your 5 favorite emotions to experience?

1. _____   4. _____

2. _____   5. _____

3. _____

4. When is the last time you experienced one or more of these 5 positive emotions? Explain what happened.

_____

_____

_____

5. What are the 5 things that you are most grateful for today?

_____

_____

Tomorrow I choose:

_____

Day #349

1. When is the last time you felt jealous? Explain what happened.

_____

_____

2. How does jealousy or envy negatively affect your life? Explain.

_____

_____

_____

3. When in the past week have you felt the most at peace with your life? Explain what was going on.

_____

_____

_____

4. Is feeling peaceful valuable to your well-being? Explain why or why not.

_____

_____

_____

5. What are the 5 things that you are most grateful for today?

_____

_____

Tomorrow I choose:

_____

Day #350

1. Would you consider yourself a good decision maker? Explain why or why not.

_____

_____

_____

2. What is the best decision you recently made? Explain.

_____

_____

3. What is the worst decision you recently made? Explain.

_____

_____

_____

4. What have you learned from making both good and bad decisions?

_____

_____

_____

5. What are the 5 things that you are most grateful for today?

_____

_____

Tomorrow I choose:

_____

Day #351

1. If you could eliminate one limitation in your life what would it be and why?

_____

_____

2. How do you believe that your life would change if this limitation were eliminated? Explain.

_____

_____

_____

3. How can weaknesses or limitations serve you in a positive way? Explain.

_____

_____

_____

4. What is one previous weakness that you have turned into a strength? Explain.

_____

_____

_____

5. What are the 5 things that you are most grateful for today?

_____

_____

Tomorrow I choose:

_____

Day #352

1. What qualities make a mom a good mom? Explain.

_____

_____

_____

2. What qualities make a dad a good dad? Explain.

_____

_____

_____

3. What is your most inspiring quality? Explain what it is and why?

_____

_____

4. What is a quality that you appreciate in others that you are working on improving within yourself and why?

_____

_____

_____

5. What are the 5 things that you are most grateful for today?

_____

_____

Tomorrow I choose:

_____

Day #353

1. What statement of encouragement would feel really good to hear today?

_____

_____

2. If you could say something encouraging to a friend or peer, what would you say and to whom?

_____

_____

3. What is something courageous you have done or tried that you are most proud of? Explain.

_____

_____

_____

4. Would you be willing to give the shirt off your back to someone in need? Share why or why not.

_____

_____

_____

5. What are the 5 things that you are most grateful for today?

_____

_____

Tomorrow I am committed to:

_____

Day #354

1. What do you like best about your life right now? Explain what is going right.

_____

_____

2. What do you like least about your life right now? Explain what is difficult.

_____

_____

_____

3. Do you find yourself more focused on what you like best or what you like least? Explain.

_____

_____

4. How do you feel when you focus on the good things as opposed to the bad things going on in your life?

_____

_____

_____

5. What are the 5 things that you are most grateful for today?

_____

_____

Tomorrow I choose:

_____

Day #355

1. Do you find it difficult to admit when you are wrong? Explain why or why not.

_____

_____

_____

2. On a scale of 1 to 10 (10 being the most), how argumentative would you say you are? Explain your answer.

_____

_____

3. On a scale of 1 to 10 (10 being the most), how understanding would you say you are? Explain your answer.

_____

_____

4. If you could go on an adventure anywhere in the world, where would you go, what would you do, and who would you bring with you? Give details.

_____

_____

_____

5. What are the 5 things that you are most grateful for today?

_____

_____

Tomorrow I choose:

_____

Day #356

1. Do you believe you are worthy of good things? Explain why or why not.

_____

_____

2. What is your biggest insecurity? Explain.

_____

_____

_____

3. How does this insecurity affect your life? Give examples.

_____

_____

_____

4. What are your 5 most amazing qualities that remind you of how great you are?

1. _____   4. _____

2. _____   5. _____

3. _____

5. What are the 5 things that you are most grateful for today?

_____

_____

Tomorrow I choose:

_____

Day #357

1. Have you been the kind of friend that you want as a friend? Explain.

_____

_____

2. Are your closest friends the kind of friends that lift you up or bring you down? Explain.

_____

_____

3. What mistake have you learned the most from? What happened, and what did you learn?

_____

_____

_____

4. Do you have a difficult time being accountable for the mistakes you make? Explain in detail why or why not.

_____

_____

_____

5. What are the 5 things that you are most grateful for today?

_____

_____

Tomorrow I choose:

_____

Day #358

1. Do you get more energized by spending time alone or spending time with others? Explain the energy difference.

_____

_____

_____

_____

2. What are the 10 most helpful things you have learned about yourself doing this journal?

1. _____

2. _____

3. _____

4. _____

5. _____

6. _____

7. _____

8. _____

9. _____

10. _____

(continued on the next page...)

Day #358, continued

3. What is one area where you have felt an incredible improvement in your life? Explain.

_____

_____

_____

4. What recent conversation has impacted you the most and why? Explain the situation and with whom you were talking to.

_____

_____

_____

5. What are the 5 things that you are most grateful for today?

_____

_____

_____

Tomorrow I choose:

_____

_____

Day #359

1. What has caused you to feel sad recently? Explain.

_____

_____

2. On a scale of 1 to 10 (10 being the best), how have you done with accepting your sadness into your heart? Explain your scoring and what your experience has been.

_____

_____

3. How do you handle sadness, anger, or frustration? Do you communicate well? Do you stay calm? Do you lose your temper? Do you hold your feelings in? Explain.

_____

_____

_____

4. What are 3 things that you would enjoy doing with your family?

1. _____

2. _____

3. _____

5. What are the 5 things that you are most grateful for today?

_____

_____

Tomorrow I choose:

_____

Day #360

1. What are 3 goals that you are currently working on?

1. _____

2. _____

3. _____

2. What was the last goal that you set and accomplished?

_____

_____

3. What emotions do you experience when you accomplish something you have set out to do?

_____

_____

_____

4. Where do you struggle the most with goal setting? Explain.

_____

_____

_____

5. What are the 5 things that you are most grateful for today?

_____

_____

Tomorrow I choose:

_____

Day #361

1. Have you ever been wrongly accused of something? If so, explain what happened. If not, explain how you imagine it would feel to be wrongly accused of something.

_____

_____

_____

2. What is a current event that is happening that upsets you? Explain.

_____

_____

3. If you could do something to impact this current event, what would you do?

_____

_____

_____

4. How would it feel to make this kind of difference in the world and why?

_____

_____

_____

5. What are the 5 things that you are most grateful for today?

_____

_____

Tomorrow I choose:

_____

Day #362

1. Do you believe that you are capable of greatness? Explain why or why not.

_____

_____

2. What does being great mean to you? Explain.

_____

_____

_____

3. Who do you believe is the greatest person who has ever lived and why?

_____

_____

_____

4. What attributes about this person inspire you the most?

_____

_____

_____

5. What are the 5 things that you are most grateful for today?

_____

_____

Tomorrow I choose:

_____

Day #363

1. What keeps you up at night? Explain anything that you overthink or worry about.

_____

_____

_____

2. What are a few ways that you have learned to calm your worries?

_____

_____

3. What is your strongest sense (taste, touch, smell, sound, sight) and what do you appreciate most about it?

_____

_____

4. If you could fly for the day, where would you go and what would you want to see? Explain.

_____

_____

_____

5. What are the 5 things that you are most grateful for today?

_____

_____

Tomorrow I choose:

_____

Day #364

1. What is the most invaluable wisdom you have gained over the past year? Explain.

_____

_____

_____

2. How have you improved as a person over the past year?

_____

_____

3. What have been your 3 proudest moments over the past 365 days?

1. _____

2. _____

3. _____

4. How happy does your heart feel in general compared to when you started this journal?

_____

_____

_____

5. What are the 5 things that you are most grateful for today?

_____

_____

Tomorrow I choose:

_____

Day #365

1. What is the most powerful message you want to tell yourself today that will help you through your days ahead?

_____

_____

_____

_____

2. What are your 10 best qualities that you value the most?

1. I am: _____

2. I am: _____

3. I am: _____

4. I am: _____

5. I am: _____

6. I am: _____

7. I am: _____

8. I am: _____

9. I am: _____

10. I am: _____

♡ Tip: This is something that you should read and reflect on regularly. It will help you to stay in your happy heart and remain connected to your life.

(continued on the next page...)

Day #365, continued

3. Write a letter to one person who you would like to thank for being supportive of you over the past 365 days.

_____

_____

_____

_____

4. Write a letter to yourself describing what you have accomplished and learned while writing this journal; as well as your vision, commitments, hopes, and goals for the next 365 days. ♡

_____

_____

_____

_____

5. What are the 5 things that you are most grateful for today?

_____

_____

_____

Tomorrow I choose:

_____

_____

_____

INSTRUCTIONS

1. Draw a large heart on the page provided.

2. Somewhere on the page write your 5 most treasured and prioritized personal values or attributes—your top "I am…" statements. If possible say each "I am" aloud and really feel it. If you say them in your mind, make sure to feel it there too.

3. On another part of the page, write 5 "I feel…" statements, which will correlate to one of your 5 "I am's." For example, if you said, "I am kind," you would take a moment to feel how it feels to know you are kind and in turn write what you feel as a response. For example, "I feel warm," or "I feel proud of myself." Whatever it is you feel in that moment. Do this so you have 5 "I feel's" connected to each "I am."

4. Next, you will draw lines in your heart to separate 5 different heart map lines (see example below) and write one of your "I am's" in each of the 5 spots in your heart. Color them with whatever colors inspire you!

6. Write your "I feel's" along the perimeter of the outside of your heart. These feelings will serve to remind you to protect your connection with your Happy Heart.

7. Have fun, feel it, and be creative!

Example Happy Heart
by Royce Rielly

Draw your happy heart here!

About the Author

Lindsay Rielly is the founder of Live Your Standard and The Happy Heart Program, which are transformational, life-application programs that effectively guide clients into purposeful and joyful living; thriving opposed to surviving; emotional literacy; personal healing and overall optimal health and well-being. She graduated summa cum laude from the University of California, Los Angeles, with a degree in Gender Studies and specialties in psychology, sociology, and communications. Rielly is a published author, award-winning executive producer and owner of Continuum Entertainment, an entertainment firm with over nineteen years of talent management, branding, and event production experience. She has dedicated much of her life to causes that serve the less fortunate with a particular passion for empowering children to become self-accepting, compassionate, and purposeful individuals.